Human Station in the Bahá'í Faith

Selected Sections: Philosophy and Knowledge of the Divine

Human Station in the Bahá'í Faith

Selected Sections: Philosophy and Knowledge of the Divine

Dr. 'A. M. Dávúdí

The original Persian edition was compiled and published by: Dr. Vahid Ra'fatí

Translated by: Riaz Masrour

JUXTA PUBLISHING LIMITED | HONG KONG

For my beloved sons, Nader and Shapour, in recognition of their
passionate and abiding service to the Cause of Bahá'u'lláh

Table of Contents

Foreword

This book is a collection of talks by the great Bahá'í teacher and philosopher Dr. 'A. M. Dávúdí on selected philosophical topics. A member of the Iranian National Spiritual Assembly during the Iranian revolution, Dr. Dávúdí was abducted by unknown assailants while strolling in a park in Tehran in 1979 and was never heard from again.

Since the inception of the Bahá'í Faith some 169 years ago in Iran and its announcement by Bahá'u'lláh, the Founder of the Faith, the Bahá'ís of Iran have been the subject of unceasing persecution and constant torment. They have been vilified, denigrated and considered to be idol worshippers deserving of imprisonment, torture and death. Multitudes have been imprisoned, untold numbers of Bahá'í homes and properties, including places of worship, historical sites and even cemeteries, have been expropriated and destroyed. In these 169 years, a great many Bahá'ís have been murdered for their religious beliefs. The horror continues today.

An implacable orthodoxy governing the country is determined to eradicate its Bahá'í community, the largest religious minority of Iran. The Bahá'ís believe in the fundamental unity of all religions and therefore consider themselves to be members of a universal family. Their goal is to unite peoples of all ethnicities, nationalities, and religious backgrounds in an effort to achieve world peace.

The clerical establishment is absent in the Bahá'í Faith. Thus the administration of Bahá'í affairs is in the hands of elected institutions referred to as *Spiritual Assemblies*. These Assemblies are composed of nine members and are elected annually from the rank and file of the believers. There are local and national Spiritual Assemblies responsible for the administration and coordination of all affairs in each city and country respectively. The world governing body of the Faith, *the Universal House of Justice*, is located in Haifa, Israel and its members are elected every five years by the worldwide Bahá'í community in a two-step process.

Dr. Dávúdí was a member of the National Spiritual Assembly of Iran in 1979 when the Iranian revolution broke out. The entire membership of the Assembly was arrested, found guilty of the charge of "source of corruption on earth" and was summarily executed. Dr. Dávúdí had already been abducted at this time and assumed to have been murdered. A second elected National Spiritual Assembly membership met the same fate. Since the formation of any Bahá'í administrative body was ruled unlawful by the Iranian government, the Universal House of Justice (in compliance with the principle of obedience to the Iranian laws) directed the Bahá'í community to desist from forming a new National Spiritual Assembly. Alternatively, a seven-member body referred to as the *Yárán* (friends), was formed and was allowed to function by government authorities in order to conduct the day-to-day business of the Bahá'í community. Although all of its communications and directives were transparent and reviewable by the authorities, yet abruptly and without provocation, the entire group was arrested in early 2008, and charged with spying for foreign powers and is currently languishing in prison, victims of a 20-year sentence.

Dr. Dávúdí's works are numerous and varied. The original Persian version of his talks contained in this volume were compiled and edited by Dr. Vahid Ra'fati, a close associate of Dr. Dávúdí and currently the head of the research department at the Bahá'í World Centre. The Persian version of this book was published by Kalimat Press in 1987. There are other volumes of his talks that have also been published in the original Persian and are currently available for purchase. It should be noted that despite their clarity and eloquence of presentation, all scholarly works such as those produced by Dr. Dávúdí, remain provisional in nature and should be regarded by the readers as an attempt by the authors to offer their understanding of a concept or provide elucidation for an otherwise complex or abstruse topic related to Bahá'í Writings. Bahá'í scholarship offers a wide arena of intellectual activity in which scholars are free to express their views and thoughts regarding Bahá'í principles or concepts. However, these remain personal views and should not be considered as authoritative statements of Bahá'í beliefs.

In 2005, Mrs. Dávúdí, currently living in Canada, expressed an interest in having an English translation of the works of her beloved husband published so that English-speaking friends may be able to read and enjoy his presentation of the many interesting and at times complex topics which abound in the Bahá'í scripture. It is a pity that his oral presentations cannot be duplicated in English so that the Western friends might enjoy the fluidity of his expression, the wonderful eloquence of his speech, the elegance of his diction and the crystal clear elucidation of the subject under consideration. No one could come away from one of his sessions without a complete understanding of the subject. He satisfied the mind and touched the heart. He left no unanswered questions.

Mrs. Dávúdí's request was transmitted to me by my sister Forouzandeh Masrour, a close friend of Mrs. Dávúdí, and I took it upon myself to attempt the rather difficult task of producing a translation, which would not only remain Faithful to the literal rendering of the concepts but also deliver, to the extent possible, the inimitable beauty and force of the original.

The original Persian edition of this work consists of 19 talks. The current English version contains 13 of the topics which I felt would be of specific interest to the Western readers. However, I have included the translation of another of his talks that is not part of this work but is critically important in the current political climate. His speech on the subject of the non-political nature of the Bahá'í Faith and the non-involvement of the believers in partisan politics seemed to me to be of special significance. Although it was presented to a Persian audience over 30 years ago, yet the basic principles are clearly relevant now.

These are verbal presentations which have been transcribed and now translated into English. As was Dr. Dávúdí's approach, he would repeat certain concepts using different word constructs in order to illuminate the subject matter. In some cases I have taken the liberty to either shorten a paragraph or lengthen it by including additional verbiage in order to tighten the content or make it more understandable to a Western reader. In no case has the meaning or intention of the speaker been altered.

I am hopeful that in the near future the remaining addresses of the present work as well as some of the other works of Dr. Dávúdí may be rendered into English so that the English- speaking friends may get to know and love this great man of intellect whose devotion to the Faith of Bahá'u'lláh could not be compromised even at the price of his life. We, who knew him, were taught by him and loved him, will continue to feel his absence and consider his services to the Faith and his ultimate sacrifice as an evidence of the wondrous beauty and grandeur of the Cause of Bahá'u'lláh and Dr. Dávúdí himself as an unforgettable exemplar of its teachings. It is to the imperishable memory of that unforgettable spirit that this work is dedicated.

Riaz Masrour, December of 2012

A Short Biography of Dr. 'A.M. Dávúdí

A prominent scholar and philosopher and a beloved author of numerous Bahá'í works, 'Alí-Murád Dávúdí was born in Khalkhál, Azerbaijan, in 1921. He was raised in a Bahá'í family renowned for its devotion to the Cause and the recipient of several tablets from 'Abdu'l-Bahá and the Guardian.

In an interview, in response to the question regarding his activities in his youth, Dr. Dávúdí spoke the following words:

> I must tell you that I practically skipped over my youth. I don't say this as a recommendation for others to follow; I mention this to merely indicate that my personality and disposition was that of an introvert, causing me to outgrow my youth much too quickly and before my time. In fact today I feel much younger than the way I felt during those early years. In that time span I seldom felt happy or showed any interest in play, sports or other recreations. I spent my time reading and studying. And again I don't mean to portray this attitude as a virtue. I simply mean that study was a sort of escape or a refuge for me as I was, by nature, rather withdrawn. It was not that the love of reading led to my seclusion or aloofness but rather I read because I was a hermit at heart.

> Of course I am not too unhappy about the intellectual activities of my youth since it is generally agreed that if young people remain idle they may be tempted to involve themselves in other forms of

entertainment which may prove to be inappropriate, unhealthy or even dangerous. Moreover, this lifestyle suited me well since at that time, I owned and administrated a large country estate which employed a variety of laborers and craftsmen and as the administrator of the estate I was actually expected to remain aloof from those who lived and worked on the property. This and other issues combined to promote in me an attitude of self-reliance and accustomed me to a lonely life which kept me from serving the Faith the way I should have, although I had done better in my childhood. So, in my years of early manhood as I remained uninterested in most activities, I also failed to participate in the service to the Cause. For me, this failure remains a source of deep regret for having missed the opportunity to serve the Faith when I had the chance to do so.

After completing his high school education, Dávúdí moved to Tehran, was accepted in the university and began his studies in the fields of Persian and Arabic literature, Iranian and Islamic history and Eastern and Western philosophy. He became well-known among the students and professors as a bright and diligent young man, and remained a favorite of both groups. After receiving his degree, he was employed by the Ministry of Education as a teacher of languages and literature at high schools in a number of provincial cities. While working in Zanján in 1952, he married Malakih Áfáq Iránpúr. The Dávúdís had five children who followed in their father's footsteps in serving the Cause in various fields.

Following several years of teaching in the provinces, Dávúdí moved to Tehran and continued his education at the University of Tehran while teaching in high schools in the capital city. His postgraduate work was completed in France where he received his doctoral degree in Philosophy and began his teaching work at the University of Tehran as an associate professor. This led to a thirty- year career in educating young generations in literature, history, philosophy, and research methodology. During this time, he also published numerous articles and translated a number of books on philosophy from French into Persian.

After many years of service to the Cause as a member of various committees, in 1974 in the thirty-ninth gathering of the National Bahá'í Convention, Dr. Dávúdí was elected to membership on the National Spiritual Assembly of the Bahá'ís of Iran. In 1975 he was again elected to that body and was also elected secretary of the Assembly; this office placed him at the forefront of service to the Cause and to the Iranian Bahá'í community. In his years of service as the secretary of the National Spiritual Assembly he traveled widely and visited numerous local Bahá'í Assemblies and communities, spoke to many individuals resolving personal problems and inspiring the friends and local Assemblies in their service. In each case he was received with a rousing welcome by the friends, and when he spoke to them at gatherings, he helped enrich the spiritual atmosphere of the gatherings by his eloquent and captivating words.

In 1978, Dr. Dávúdí, along with the other members of the National Assembly, traveled to the Holy Land and attended the fourth Bahá'í International Convention in Haifa, where as a pilgrim, he visited the Bahá'í holy sites and placed his forehead on the threshold of the shrine of Bahá'u'lláh. In Haifa he also learned of the remarkable successes of other National Assemblies and the important contributions of friends all around the world.

In Iran, Dr. Dávúdí served on the committee for the collection, coordination and publication of the Bahá'í Scriptures. He also reviewed, edited and reorganized the works of various Bahá'í authors prior to their publication. One of his most significant contributions as a member of the committee for the distribution of Bahá'í literature was his leading role in preparing and publishing a series of 18 publications called *The Study of Bahá'í Literature* in which a detailed description of the Bahá'í principles and beliefs supported by passages from the Sacred Writings were presented. The goal of such publications was to shed light on the many misunderstandings and misrepresentations that were rampant in the media and among the Iranian people, and to provide compelling

3

responses to longstanding questions regarding the nature and purpose of the Bahá'í Faith and its relationship to Islam.

Perhaps Dr. Dávúdí's most important service to the Bahá'í community and especially to the Bahá'í youth was the establishment of courses of study that he presented in summer schools and various deepening classes for the education of the young and eager Bahá'ís. This effort reached its peak with his classes at the Bahá'í Institute of Higher Learning. The creation of the Bahá'í Institute of Higher Learning was one of the goals of the 5-Year Plan for the Iranian Bahá'í community as specified by the Universal House of Justice in 1975. The message of the House of Justice which called for the establishment of such a school states, "The education of a number of talented youth who have the interest, ability and fortitude required for study and research into traditional religious sciences and Holy Scriptures is essential."

In order to realize this goal, the Bahá'í Institute of Higher Learning was established in 1976 and began its work with the goal of encouraging and reinforcing the spirit of study and research in the Bahá'í Writings among the youth and training those talented minds in the principles and concepts of various religious traditions. The creation, scheduling, supervision and management of the Institute was entrusted by the National Assembly to Dr. Dávúdí, Badí'u'lláh Faríd and a few other scholars. In addition to his other responsibilities, Dr. Dávúdí was appointed to teach subjects that related to philosophy and Gnosticism (*'irfán*). For the first time in a Bahá'í school, the study of non-Bahá'í works, religious or literary, became part of the school's curriculum; Dr. Dávúdí began the process of educating his young pupils in the religious and philosophical precepts of other religions, especially Islam.

Dr. Dávúdí's enduring services to Bahá'í scholarship and culture is also reflected in the numerous articles and countless talks he gave at different venues. It is not possible to place a limit on the influence and the lasting effect of his services in all that he wrote or uttered; most of these articles and transcriptions of talks have been collected and published in the original language. Dr. Dávúdí has bequeathed to future generations a precious legacy which demonstrates his knowledge and eloquence in explaining the spiritual teachings of the Cause and its historical development. He discloses many acts of oppression, maltreatment and persecutions suffered by the followers of Bahá'u'lláh in the first decades of the second century of the Bahá'í history in Iran.

His articles written on Bahá'í philosophy and theology are, undoubtedly, the most comprehensive studies of the subject. At the top of this list are two lengthy treatises on the subject of *Divinity and Oneness.* In these two works, the foundational beliefs of the Bahá'í Faith, namely, the impossibility of knowing the Divine Being and the position and role of the Manifestation of God, are elucidated. His arguments are supported by passages from the tablets of Bahá'u'lláh which are compiled and presented in a systematic and convincing manner. Dávúdí utilizes an elevated yet effective style and offers proof from the Writings with such clarity that no one whose heart is pure and whose mind is free from prejudice can object to or deny his arguments.

The fundamental principle that is consistently emphasized by Dr. Dávúdí in his numerous Writings, is that the mere study and understanding of the Bahá'í Writings is not an end, in itself, for the Bahá'í community. The only path of service that can open the channels of divine confirmation and guarantee ultimate success is teaching and pioneering. What is considered significant to Dávúdí, a concept that he constantly stresses in his Writings, is that the time in which we live is the period for pioneering and teaching; it is the time to arise and share the Bahá'í teachings with those who seek. This is a time when amassing of knowledge of the Writings should only serve as the first step on the path to becoming a teacher of the Cause to the waiting world. The time for philosophical and scientific discussions, delving into mystical and enigmatic verses in the Writings and rigorous research of various complex and abstruse details of the tablets will come. Today, such scholarly efforts must be accompanied by actions required to facilitate and expedite, ever increasingly, the teaching work and spreading of the message of Bahá'u'lláh.

Since Dr. Dávúdí's field of study was philosophy and he had, for many years, trained his students in the methodology of scientific research, his works are all clearly supported by the use of logic and the application of intellect and reason on all issues. Although he draws from logical tools of the intellect, he does so with support of his power of Faith. The harmony and reconciliation between intellect and emotion, between logic and spiritual attraction that flows from the power of Faith can be seen in what he has written or uttered.

His strong views regarding the quality of Bahá'í publications and magazines confirm his opinion that all such works must be well-written using an elevated form of expression and that the sublimity of such exposition should not be compromised. The author should not try to produce works consonant with popular and prevalent writing formats in order to satisfy the general readers' expectations. In an interview he explains:

> I disagree with the idea that the level of literary excellence of Bahá'í works should be reduced to make them understandable to the general reader. On the contrary, the knowledge and literary capability of the friends, especially the youth must be enhanced such that they can develop a better understanding of the Bahá'í concepts as they are presented. We cannot express the novel and sublime notions of the Faith using common, colloquial or popular language as they will then lose their essential effect and become something other than what they were intended to be.

Dr. Dávúdí set forth the purpose, goals and methodology of Bahá'í education and moral training in an important article, a portion of which follows:

> The biggest mistake of an educator is to try to find a non-religious basis for moral instruction of his pupils and assume that moral virtues and human rectitude of conduct can be taught to children through any approach other than through teaching of religious principles and spiritual qualities.
>
> It is not seemly to forgo the principles and teachings of the Faith and follow the whims and ever-changing fancies of the scholars and intellectuals or imitate the social trends and the passing fads, and in so doing lose our way and our identity. If we consider ourselves Bahá'ís and are devoted to principles of the Faith of Bahá'u'lláh, we must accept His precept that the moral education of children must start with the basic principles of belief in God and in His religion.

In another section of the article, he writes:

> Physical and material education is necessary to support spiritual training. A Bahá'í must be healthy, strong and prosperous so that he is enabled to utilize this health, strength and wealth in the path of service to the cause of humanity and if we look closely, the true meaning of spirituality is nothing else but this. A Bahá'í child whether boy or girl should not be raised in conditions of utter comfort, ease and complacency since his work will entail traversing many roads, passing through jungles, scaling mountains and crossing oceans. His purpose will be breaking the chains of prejudice, removing the fetters of enmity, freeing the slaves of superstition, quenching the fire of violence and war and uniting the human family of whatever religion, color, race and country. Such difficult tasks cannot be expected from men or women who seek lives of comfort and pleasure.

Dr. Dávúdí was a noble and earnest man with a disciplined mind and unpretentious ways. He was well-liked, well-spoken and extremely courteous and easily impressed and moved by matters that involved human emotions and feelings. To these virtues, his Bahá'í and non-Bahá'í students, university colleagues and his friends and acquaintances, young and old and from whatever creed or ideology, bear witness.

Dr. Vahíd Ra'fatí, who met Dr. Dávúdí in the summer of 1977 at the offices of the National Spiritual Assembly of Iran, recalls,

> He welcomed and embraced me with indescribable feelings of affection and love. Rather than sitting in his chair behind the desk, he sat right next to me and inquired about the progress of my university education and successes in my Bahá'í activities. As I shared with him the nature of my work, he offered words of praise and approval. Only God knows the extent to which he showed interest in the Bahá'í youth's upholding of the principles of the Cause of God and their scientific and intellectual development.

Dr. Dávúdí himself writes: "To the youth, we submit our hearts and our hopes, and in them we seek our longings and goals. I wish that the youth will continue to keep our hopeful and yearning hearts brimming with yet to be achieved hopes and still to come victories."

The youth, too, loved him dearly. One of his students who could be expressing the thoughts and feelings of all of his students writes: "...they loved him so and called him *ustád* (master) and shed tears at the conclusion of each class as he walked away."

Another student writes: "He visited Mashhad in the summer of 1349sh (1970). The Bahá'í youth who had, for years, been the target of anti-Bahá'í slander and malice and the subject of the darts of prejudice and hatred of the malevolent, were overjoyed to receive him, attended all of his sessions such that a single empty seat could hardly be found in the hall, and listened to him with rapt attention. Such a reception for the two full weeks was entirely unprecedented."

And another youth writes: "I swear that the light of Faith and belief in the Cause of God shone in my heart due to his words; words that were infused with the love of God and were devoid of any trace of bias or prejudice. I don't know the present situation of that wonderful and noble man, but I entreat God to keep him safe and grant us another opportunity of meeting him."

Dr. Dávúdí's destiny was to be placed in the forefront of the struggle to defend the principles and precepts of the Faith during the most turbulent and dangerous times in the history of the Cause of God. It fell to him to console and inspire the persecuted Iranian Bahá'ís, encourage and energize them and write reports and entreaties to government authorities appealing for justice and fair play regarding the rights of the Bahá'í citizens of Iran. It seems as if Dr. Dávúdí had amassed his knowledge, experience and wisdom, over the years, in order to put them to use with great courage and audacity in defense of all that is sacred in the Cause and also to unmask the many acts of violence and brutality inflicted upon the harassed and oppressed Bahá'í community of Iran.

His niece writes:

> Right at the time when the storm of calamity and adversity raged fiercely and the black clouds of enmity and hatred bore signs of darker days to come, Dr. Dávúdí, confidently, serenely and with his customary air of dignity and grace, gave the friends lessons in perseverance and confidence and at the same time prepared himself as he approached, with open arms, his ineluctable destiny. A few days prior to his abduction he confided to one of his close relatives these words: "In the path of the Blessed Beauty [Bahá'u'lláh], I have experienced but little adversity. I have not even received a slap in the face in the path of service to the Cause; I pray that I will be given the opportunity to attain the gift of calamity in His path."

Regarding those days, Zohreh, Dr. Dávúdí's daughter writes:

> In April of 1979, a few months after the revolution, I returned to Iran to plead with my father to leave Iran for the U.S. or Canada. My father would not have any of it and explained that the Iranian Bahá'í youth needed him and that if he were to leave Iran, many would lose heart and the courage to endure. This was true as our

phone rang constantly all day long and my father would speak with the friends and share with them words of consolation and encouragement. Several times we received calls telling us that they were coming to arrest my father. Despite my tearful pleas, he simply packed his pajamas, razor, cologne, and a prayer-book and placed the bag next to his bed and waited. At no time did he show any signs of worry or even concern, and I will never forget his smile under such conditions. I carry with me many sweet and bitter memories of those times, and as I remember the anguish and anxieties that dominated our hearts, I feel great pride for having had a father such as 'Alí ján.

And so, it was the destiny of the oppressed and tormented Iranian Bahá'í community in that volatile period of its history to be robbed of such a scholar and a man of such devotion and courage.

The cowardly enemies of the Faith that considered his elimination from the arena of defending the principles and sacred tenets of the Cause of God as a major victory for themselves and a grave and irreparable loss for the Iranian Bahá'í Community, abducted him as he strolled in a park near his house on Nov. 11, 1979, and despite all efforts made to locate his whereabouts, he was never found. Sometime later the newspaper, *Front of Freedom* publishing an article titled "Dr. Dávúdí, University Professor, was abducted" wrote:

> It is now two weeks since the abduction of Dr. Dávúdí, a professor at Tehran University. He had left his home for a stroll in the nearby Láleh Park when he disappeared, and despite a long and exhaustive search, no news of him is discovered. It is presumed that he has been abducted. It would be better for the responsible authorities to provide any information they may have regarding his whereabouts as a humanitarian act. We strongly object to the abduction of individuals for whatever reason.

Five months later, at Ridván 1980, when the Iranian Bahá'í Community elected its National Assembly, Dr. Dávúdí was elected *in absentia*. The community showed that they loved him, understood and appreciated his merits and sacrifice, and stood firm in their loyalty to him.

1. Preface: The Basic Beliefs of the People of Bahá

The selected topic of this chapter is the Beliefs of the People of Bahá. Of course only the subject highlights are discussed here since any attempt at detailed treatment of the subject would require separate presentations of various principles and tenets of the Bahá'í Faith. Therefore this chapter will only concern itself with a discussion of the salient features of the core "beliefs" of the Bahá'í Faith.

The definition of the word "belief" requires that its meaning and implications be carefully considered. Belief is a word that denotes obedience and adherence, and yet also takes in elements of freedom of choice and will. It depicts at once a state of conviction and attachment and yet also of choice and freedom. Belief therefore is a state of voluntary binding of a believer to a set of principles. This implies that a believer is one who of and by himself has agreed to become bound to a certain belief. This of course is different from being compelled into obedience; with compulsive belief the participant has not freely agreed to obey but does so because he has to. In the Bahá'í definition, coercion and constraint, reward and punishment remain alien to the concept of belief as the word implies that the believer, having once acknowledged his beliefs accepts to be bound by them and that if he had not wished to do so he would have been free not to believe.

1. Preface: The Basic Beliefs of the People of Bahá

Acceptance of beliefs is the agreement to be bound and therefore he who believes requires no compulsion. No punishment can coerce him. It is he who accepts to be bound and allows the harness around his neck. And once he accepts the harness, he is freed from every other restriction. Its effect on him is the same, whether in public or private, whether in fear or leisure; once the harness is worn he begins to experience peace. In other words he finds comfort in this bondage because thereafter he no longer asks: "what should I do?" "Where should I go?" "Where should I stay?" as the strap around his neck will keep him in the direction that is best for him, sends him where he wants to go and stops him from where he should not venture. And because of this he finds peace of mind; his anxiety dissipates, and he no longer asks: "what should I do?" This peace that emerges from such a state is also known as "faith", which implies peace due to reliance and devotion. Belief brings faith, which in turn brings peace of mind, dispels anxiety and shows the way forward; that obligation is not an imposition since the wearing of the harness has been a voluntary act.

Accepting a belief system is different from imitation. Imitation also entails harness and chain but it is more similar to placing a leash around a dog's neck and pulling it along. He who imitates does not willingly accept to become attached or to become bound, but rather he abandons his intellect and common sense so that his leash may be controlled by someone else. Belief is associated with main principles, but imitation, even in those religions which sanction it, applies to secondary teachings. In those religions, too, principles are accepted on the basis of actual belief in them. In other words one actually accepts to be bound by them and consequently experiences peace and freedom. "I have been free from the day I was bound to Thee."

Thus a collection of beliefs is a set of principles that man agrees to be bound by and remains Faithful to. Man desires this bondage with heart and soul and accepts it willingly and with pleasure and yet if he did not accept it nothing would happen and no apparent problem would arise. If such a problem does exist in other religions, it ceases to exist in the Bahá'í Faith since its Founder has taught that His Faith should be accepted willingly and joyfully and with absolute freedom. This concept is being emphasized here to highlight the fact that those who investigate this Cause should realize that the nature and concept of freedom of belief is an indispensible principle of this Faith. Nowhere else has such a measure of freedom been sanctioned as in the Bahá'í Faith. Once a child reaches the age of maturity, he of his own volition must agree to become a Bahá'í otherwise he will not be considered a Bahá'í. Is it possible that a Muslim child would say that he is not a Muslim? According to the rules of Islam, his punishment would be the shedding of his blood. In other Faiths, abandoning one's belief system is also regarded with some measure of disdain. It is only in the Bahá'í Faith, the most recent of the great religions which has emerged at the time of man's intellectual and spiritual maturity, that such a thing has become possible; no one may be considered a believer unless at the age of maturity he freely and willingly admits to such a belief. And even then he continues to maintain the right to remove his name from the list of believers anytime he so desires. In former times how could anyone imagine that a believer could decide to disavow his beliefs and announce that he no longer wishes to remain within the fold and actually possess the freedom to do so?

Therefore to sum up: the collection of principles that we agree to adhere to as the basis of our belief system has not been imposed upon us; our following the principles is not the result of imitation; no one has put a leash around our neck since we have of our own volition agreed to accept them[1].

---

[1] This is a reference to a story in the book *Kitáb-i-Bústán* by the great Persian poet Sa'dí. The book has not been translated into English.

Belief that leads to Faith completes its journey in love. The highest level of Faith is love. Until Faith completes itself in love it remains deficient. Belief, Faith and piety find their ultimate reality in love. A lover is attached to his beloved. He is utterly helpless to do other than to act according to the dictates of love, and yet he is not compelled to love as it is he himself who has accepted to wear the harness of love. He carries the burden of love with pleasure. As the poet says: "He considers it a favor who carries the burden of love" as the burden he carries on his shoulder is to him a benevolent gift. Bahá'u'lláh has said: "Observe My commandment for the love of My beauty".[2] The basis for observing the commandments is belief. And this belief, as required by this verse, must be a sign of love. Where there are whispers of: "why am I doing this?", or when obedience to commandments becomes a resented obligation, the signs of Faith disappear. One must with all his heart and soul be drawn to this voluntary observance. One must do this because of one's belief, one's Faith and one's love.

A Bahá'í considers love to be the very cause of creation. Bahá'u'lláh in one of His tablets has clearly stated that love is the cause of creation.[3] Now let us see what this concept means. Why did creation come about?

The answer to this question creates conflicting arguments since regardless of the reason that one may perceive, the concept suggests a state of need or obligation on the part of God to create. In other words, since once the reason or the purpose of creation is fixed, it immediately carries with it the implication that such a purpose had not at one time been considered and that subsequently God wished to actualize it. It could be argued that detection of a certain

---

[2] *The Book of Aqdas*, p. 20.
[3] *Ad'íyih Hadrat-i-Mahbúb* (*The Prayers of the Beloved*), p. 409. This is a compilation of verses by Bahá'u'lláh, some of which have been translated into English.

deficiency in Him led to His act of creation in order to eliminate the flaw.

Obviously such a conception can in no wise be applicable to God. If we imagine God in these terms we have relegated Him from His divine and transcendent station. Therefore it is not possible to consider any other reason for creation but love. Why did God create? Because He loved to create; no other reason is necessary. You love someone and you ask yourself, "why do I love that person?" If in response to this question the thought crosses your mind that you love that person in order to achieve a certain purpose, then this is no longer love. You yourself would be the first to admit that what you feel is not love. Love is love when its only purpose is to love. I love, period. If it is anything but this, it is not love; it is for gain; it is a transaction, but it is not love.

Therefore if we wish to put forth an aim or purpose for creation, we must say that the act of creation is an act of love or that in and of itself it is love. Why did He create? Because He loved to create. He did not wish to create in order to achieve an end which could raise the question that He had not possessed that end before. Of course compared to the way we love, a sentiment that may be generally defined as "contingent love", this love can have no meaning. Love can approach that level of purity if it is devoid of hypocrisy. The love that originates in God, who is an absolute being, is of this kind. He loved to create and therefore He created. And because of this He has asked that our recognition of Him should originate out of our love to know Him and that He will admit no other avenue of access to convey to Him that recognition.

Why do we consider God as self-sufficient? Because He does not change; transition has no meaning in that heavenly realm. From a beginning that has no beginning to eternity we see Him in a state of utter constancy. Any comparison between this ever-evolving world of space and time with that eternal realm becomes impossible since change loses its meaning. Change is an indication of deficiency which has an application only in the contingent world. That absolute constancy and utter perpetuity which from the beginning that has no beginning to the end that has no end continues to exist eternally; we recognize it as the eternal kingdom and the kingdom of God. Therefore in so far as the essence of God is concerned we believe it to be in a state of absolute constancy. If we abandon this essential quality then He will be no different from the ever-changing, ever-evolving, ever-needing creatures of which He is the creator.

Thus, we believe that God is absolute constancy. Even His act of creation flows from no other purpose than wanting and loving, and therefore such acts of creation generate no change in His essence. He creates through His will, but this will to create remains constant and unchanged; His creation has existed from eternity and will exist to eternity. Our belief in the constancy of God and acceptance of the pre-existence of His essence includes also a belief in the pre-existence of His creation. If we say that there was a time when God had not begun the act of creation and then at a given time He began to create, this would imply that God had remained idle or free from the act of creation for a time and yet subsequently He again desired to create. This would mean that a change took place in Him which caused Him to stop and again start the process of creation; such a being, of and in himself, cannot be regarded as God as he has not remained within the framework of absolute constancy and eternal pre-existence.

Once we recognize God as eternal, pre-existent and immutable then we must accept that His will to create has also been eternal, pre-existent and unchanging. Where there is utter constancy, evolution has no meaning since evolution necessitates change. For creation to evolve it would mean it gradually changes and moves towards perfection. In the world of God evolution has no meaning; it is already a world of utter perfection. Neither in His essence nor His actions can evolution find application. From the beginning, which has no beginning, both He and His creation must remain at the very height of perfection.

Let us take an example:

A child wants to write. At first he writes badly; gradually he writes better and better until he begins to write well. If we say that God's original creation was imperfect and then gradually achieved perfection, then God will be not unlike the child who wrote badly but after practice learned to write better. From this it becomes essential that this creation, which is at the height of absolute perfection and is in conformity with the concept of "immutability of God's essence" was from the outset created perfect and that it serves as an example for the evolution process inherent in other grades of the creation process. This is what 'Abdu'l-Bahá has explained in *Some Answered Questions*,[4] where the matter has been treated in its entirety.

If man is the result of the evolutionary process then we must presume that God initiated His creation without the presence of man and thus imperfect and deficient and that later gradually He improved and enhanced its beauty and completeness until his perfect creation, man, emerged. Therefore man, in His perfect form, was created by God; at no time can it be imagined that the world might have been devoid of man's existence. Man has always existed since he is the most perfect creation of God. And if God had created the world of existence deficient and then had caused it to evolve towards a more perfect state, this would indicate a change in Him, which is not possible. Therefore man has always existed. It should be noted, however, that in this context "man" refers to the "Perfect Man" or the manifestation of the religion of God. The "Primal Will" which finds expression from time to time in human form is possessed of

---

[4] *Some Answered Questions,* "The Universe is Without Beginning," p. 180.

a divine spirit and is God's very original handiwork. God and His creation have always been co-existent.

God must be the Creator from the beginning and His creation, having issued from Him, must be in its perfect form. Therefore His most prefect creation, man, must have existed from the beginning that has no beginning. If we don't accept this vision then we are assuming there was a defect in the eternal process of creation.

In yet another part of *Some Answered Questions* we read that at the beginning man did not exist and that he arrived on the scene at a later time.[5] There is no conflict in these two statements. The person who exists at the beginning that has no beginning is the Manifestation of God's Faith, the Perfect Man, who comes into being in that state at the beginning and continues to exist throughout eternity without any change in His essence. In other words, the Manifestation of God's Faith in whom and from whom the Holy Spirit emanates is, like Him, eternal; is everlasting; is not born and is a single reality, which allows of no multiplicity. It is like light, which in different lamps may appear different in color and intensity and yet with these differences the reality of its oneness is not compromised. And even if these lamps are broken and the light ceases to be perceived through them, the light still exists and continues to emanate; the source of that light will continue to radiate rays of light although there is no lamp to receive the energy and transform it into usable light. The energy is still active and penetrating even though the lamp may be broken or simply turned off or otherwise prevented from manifesting the light. The Manifestation of God's Faith always exists and is the initial dispensation of God's grace even though it may not take form within a corporeal existence. When such a reality is non-existent in its corporeal form, its effect, its radiance and its intensity is even more pronounced.

---

[5] *Some Answered Questions,* "The Universe is Without Beginning," p. 180.

And so when God's Manifestation is in this world the light that emanates from Him is less penetrating than after His ascension. Once He abandons this plane of existence the power of His emanation becomes intensified. This truth has been revealed in the *Kitáb-i-Iqán*[6] and 'Abdu'l-Bahá in His interpretation of a verse of the Bible which foreshadows the coming of the Son of Man as seated upon a cloud discusses this very concept.[7] The cloud is explained as the veil between the light of the Sun and the eyes of the beholders. Since the Manifestation of God appears in the world of matter as a corporeal being with all associated physical characteristics which are barriers to His reality, it is said that He will come mounted on a cloud. The cloud prevents the light of the Sun to penetrate fully and thus the Sun's radiance and its heat become feeble.

This concept has been emphasized by 'Abdu'l-Bahá in a number of His talks. Especially after Bahá'u'lláh's ascension He repeatedly spoke on the subject and explained that the corporeal dimension of the Manifestation is like a cloud that covers the true essence of the Sun of Reality. When God's Manifestation is in this world He possesses the divine light within His physical being which hides the glory of His essence. It is very similar to the sun that shines from behind a cloud and thus its light, radiance and heat are fainter.[8] After His passing, however, the veil is lifted and His brilliance is more intense. It is on this basis that the creative word of the Manifestation finds a more profound influence after His passing than while He lives in this world.

History shows that this has always been true. Consider Jesus Christ. While He lived, the radiance of His light was so slight that none of the historians of the time made any reference to His appearance.[9]

---

[6] *Kitáb-i-Iqán*, pp. 110-111.
[7] *Some Answered Questions*, "Some Christian Subjects."
[8] *Letters of 'Abdu'l-Bahá* (Persian), vol. 4, pp. 54-59.
[9] In a tablet to Áqá Siyyid Husayn Anán, 'Abdu'l-Bahá writes: ".........Jesus Christ, may my life be a sacrifice for Him, did not gain much prominence in His

The time of Jesus' revelation was a time of civilization and a time of the emergence and expansion of Greek culture. It was not a time of fear, darkness and ignorance. On the one hand, one of the greatest civilizations known to man, the Greek civilization, was spreading its influence in the world. On the other hand, the Roman Empire with all of its power and glory had established its ascendancy in the Mediterranean region. Several great historians lived in that time and yet there is not the slightest reference to the appearance of Jesus. No one recorded that such a Faith with its teachings had been founded in Palestine. Because of this, the short-sighted historians of Europe who regard and evaluate all things and events by their physical impact and material characteristics began to doubt the revelation of the Messiah and considered Him altogether a mythical being as no intimation of his appearance could be found in any historical accounts. The emanation of His light was seemingly so feeble that other than the Bible there is no contemporary document of that time which corroborates the event of His appearance. And yet after His martyrdom we know what took place! It reached a point that today it has become the largest religion of the world in terms of its number of adherents. In historical terms it is unprecedented that any religion can reach this level of power and ascendancy. Similarly the speed by which Islam expanded its boundaries is unmatched. From the stand point of widespread expansion and penetration to peoples, tribes, and islands and various nations and races of the world, the Bahá'í Faith has no equal.

And thus the Manifestation of the religion of God, even though devoid of a physical dimension, exists and will always endure as a unique reality.

---

time. Even in the first volume of the history of Josephus, currently extant, there is no mention of the name of Christ. But in the second and especially the third edition of the book such a reference was added. In any case, due to His lack of fame, some of the philosophers of that time denied His existence...."

Referring to a number of sacred tablets, Shoghi Effendi, the Guardian of the Bahá'í Faith, emphasized the appointment of 'Abdu'l-Bahá as the Center of the Covenant that Bahá'u'lláh established with His believers. This covenant is firm and compelling, unassailable, enduring and everlasting.[10] The fundamental unity of all religions constitutes a firm and compelling teaching of our Faith. The religions of God are one. Why? Because the Manifestation of the Universal Faith of God is a single reality; every Manifestation of God from Noah to Bahá'u'lláh is the same reality. If there appear to be differences between the Manifestations of God, the differences are in the circumstances of their appearance and the relative intensity of their light. This proportional intensity is directly predicated on the capacity of the people to grasp the truth as well as the differences in their understanding of that divine reality which is immutable and does not allow multiplicity. The physical appearance of these revelators is distinctive and unique. The designation "Bahá'u'lláh", from the human point of view and with no regard to the Holy Spirit which exists within and emanates from Him, refers to the person of Bahá'u'lláh. And yet from the spiritual point of view, the word "person" loses all meaning; what exists is a single reality that exists in all religions and in all ages. The fundamentals of all religions are one and unchanging.

'Abdu'l-Bahá has emphasized that the part of religion that is considered its foundation which concerns spiritual values and moral teachings remains unchanged.[11] The spiritual foundation does not vary since its Founder is one and the same; that part of religion is the same reality. God is essential unity and absolute constancy therefore religion is also constant as it pertains to the Creator, but as it pertains to the world of humanity, religion is evolving. When you contend that religions must change and evolve, some may say: Isn't religion

---

[10] Reference to the *Lawh-i-Qarn* (Tablet of the Century) to the believers of the East, p. 101.
[11] *Some Answered Questions*, pp. 151-157.

21

from God? Then why could He not provide his complete teachings from the beginning? Why should His word continue to change? This argument is logical, and it is clear that the fundamentals of religions remain unchanged. Religion is constant and unchanging since it is associated with God, has emanated from God and God is the essence of singleness. God does not pursue a training program. In other words, He does not say something first which is deficient and then set out to gradually perfect it. Thus the word of God is fixed, firm and constant, and this is what is referred to as the foundation of all religions, unique and not subject to change. Bahá'ís understand that all religions must be considered as one. There are a number of verses in the holy Qur'an which are quite useful in teaching the Cause. These are verses which explicitly refer to the religions revealed by various Manifestations prior to the appearance of Muhammad who inaugurated the Islamic Faith. In these verses the religion inaugurated by Abraham is referred to as Islam; the religion revealed by Jesus is called Islam, Isaac's religion was referred to as Islam, Moses' religion was called Islam and Solomon's religion was called Islam. All were Moslems. All believed in Islam. There is even a verse in the Qur'an which says that should one adopt any religion but Islam, it would not be accepted of him in the sight of God. The wording is such that the "non-acceptance" is eternal.[12]

This, of course, is true since in the Qur'an God has referred to all religions before Muhammad as Islam. Applying the same logic, all religions after Him are also Islam since their realities are the same and unchanging without any conflict or difference; the realities of the religion of Abraham, that of Moses or Jesus, Mohammad or the religion of Bahá'u'lláh are all the same. Most of these religions which have been named Islam in the Qur'an have their own scriptures, their own "most sacred site", and their unique teachings. The difference in the identity of the various revelators, difference in

---

[12] Verse 85 of the Surah of Ál-i-'Irán of the Holy Qur'an

22

the names given to scriptures, different sacred locations as well as different social teachings should not be the cause of conflict between religions as their truths are one and the same. It is due to this unity of beliefs that the Qur'an calls all the religions *Islam* (The Faith), and disbelief in the Faith will not be acceptable to God.

The fundamental teachings of all religions are the same. Giving examples in spiritual matters usually produces problems and one must be careful that presentation of such examples or metaphors does not confuse the hearer rather than instruct him. In other words, it should not be thought that all aspects of any metaphor must comply with the principle under discussion. For instance it can be said that the relationship of the soul to the human body is like a ray of light which emanates from the sun and is reflected in a mirror without entering it. If the mirror breaks, the ray of light remains intact and unchanged. Questioning the validity of this metaphor, some may argue that since the light originates from the sun which is a material entity, the light (or soul) must also be material. Comparing the argument to man and his soul one can then ask how is it that the soul may not be considered material?

Although such a comparison is offered to highlight a particular aspect of an issue, the cynic may wish to apply all features of the metaphor to the concept under review which may confuse the matter and defeat the purpose. With this explanation firmly in mind we present the following comparison:

A pendulum is hanging from the ceiling. Its base at the ceiling is fixed and its end is suspended in air and is in motion. It may be possible to liken a spiritual concept to such a pendulum and propose that religion, too, has one end above and the other below. It is issued from God to be received by man. As it is issued from the kingdom of God, it is fixed, constant and unchanging and as it appears in the world of man it gains motion and change. The fundamentals of religion, or the universal realities, as they belong

23

to the divine kingdom cannot allow multiplicity and change, and yet those laws which relate to the world of man do not remain constant and unchanging. The heavenly truths, the source of which is the absolute divinity, will remain fixed and firm, and yet the social laws which have been created for man are changeable; as man evolves, the social laws are, by divine will, transformed in order to serve the requirements of the age in which they appear. In other words, the unity of God and the constancy of His Faith do not prevent the reflection of this unity and constancy in the world of man from evolving and progressing, within the limits of time and place and the prevailing conditions, and thus appearing different from religions of former ages.

Bahá'ís see no reason why these various existing religions should remain alien to each other because of differences that exist in their social teachings, manners of worship and laws. They believe that despite these differences all religions are to be considered as fundamentally one and the same because of the basic unity in their principles and basic truths. differences in the outer form of the laws of religions are not in conflict with their basic and fundamental unity.

Here is an example that can corroborate this very point. The prohibition of marriage with close relatives is among the basic laws of all religions and this prohibition has always been so. No religion sanctions marriage between close family members. And yet what is the limit of such an interdiction, and who is considered a close relative? To what extent does such a prohibition extend? These are existing differences that lend themselves to change over time. In Judaism an uncle may marry his niece. Prohibitions are applicable however to brothers and sisters and stepfathers and stepdaughters. In Islam, however, such a relationship between an uncle and his niece is prohibited, but the marriage of cousins is allowed.

So we see that the limits of the law changed without any particular rational. Why, yes to the uncle and no to the stepfather? Or why marriage of cousins is acceptable but that of uncle and niece is not acceptable? The argument has been offered by some that this has a physiological rational. This line of reasoning is unconvincing since there is common blood between cousins whereas such a problem does not exist for one's stepmother or one's stepson and yet both relationships are prohibited. Therefore the establishment of the limits of such prohibitions in past ages was never based on physiological issues or the dictates of the science of Medicine; although the subject does have both physiological and medical relevance, the limits set by religions are not necessarily in line with the findings of medical science.

In Islam the marriage of sons and daughters of aunts and uncles on both sides of the family is sanctioned and yet marrying one's aunts and uncles is prohibited. In the Bahá'í Faith the definitive limits of acceptable marriages have been left up to the Universal House of Justice, but a general guideline and main principle governing this issue is explicitly given. It is clearly stated that marriage between distant family relations is more desirable than marriage between closer ones.

This particular example is offered to show that basic realities are fixed and constant and yet their limits change over time and that one can apply the same concept to rites and observations of all religions.

Bahá'ís therefore are of the belief that the concept of constancy exists in all religions and forms the foundation that unifies all Faiths. The process of change also exists which indicates that as man changes, religions, within the limits of the time and place in which they appear, change; in light of this view point no religion can be regarded as the seal of religions. However, at the same time and based on other equally applicable principles, each religion is the seal of religions as the newly inaugurated religion is the Faith which has always existed; the reality of religions are one and the same. However in so far as their teachings and jurisdictional limits are concerned, Faiths are different from each other. These teachings and limits do not affect the reality of religion. The argument can be made that no religion can be the seal of religions since what governs mankind's existence is constant and continuous change. In relation to the world of creation, religion is an evolving process and its teachings continue to change, but in relation to God, religion is fixed and its teachings are immutable. All prophets are links of a single chain which extends from eternity to eternity and which shall never cease.

Now, we arrive at the concept that the evolutionary cycle of religion in the human world is part and parcel of the natural periodic evolutionary process. In other words religion like all other aspects of creation traverses an evolutionary and ever rising path. For example, you plant the seed, it grows to become a tree, it drives its roots into the ground and produces fruit. The fruit contains seeds, the seed fall to the earth and another tree is born. This tree evolves. In other words it sprouts, grows until it produces its fruit. However the evolution of the tree does not continue forever. It reaches its zenith of growth and then begins to decay and wither until the life process ceases, its leaves and fruits begin to fall and gradually it dries out, deteriorates and is destroyed. And yet another tree begins to sprout and go through the same growth process. Apart from the process of growth, the trees also go through a process of change. As the environmental conditions change over time, the species of trees also begin to go through a process of transformation and thus one genus of tree replaces another. Every change in this world is of this type. In other words it is created due to the motion of time. The earth turns on its axis and also moves in a straight path towards a destination which cannot be determined. The Solar system operates the same and so do the galaxies.

Spiritual matters also follow the same process. Religions go through the same transformation. Similar to all other life processes and in accordance with the natural law, a religion starts at a point, experiences a meteoric rise and stays at its zenith as long as it is destined to and then begins to decline until it reaches a point when it completely changes, and, as 'Abdu'l-Bahá teaches, no trace or sign of its civilization remains. At the same time and at another place another Faith appears.

In history, civilizations follow the same path and from age to age go through the same cycle. A civilization starts from a point, rises to the summit of its glory and then it declines and deteriorates until it dies. As it dies another civilization in another part of the world begins to bloom and grow. The Egyptian civilization, the Chinese civilization, the Indian civilization, the Greek civilization and the Persian civilization all appeared at various points in history, went through their growth cycles, reached their relative summits, shone brightly and then declined. But at the same time in another place a new civilization is founded and begins the process of its blossoming so that the cycle may continue.

The world in all its aspects works the same way. There is an age in which various epochs follow each other, reach a peak and decline until the effulgence of that age fades and is no more. The epochs remain in that state for a time and then cease to exist and their traces and effects also disappear. At the same time another age begins at another place and follows the cycle. The world of creation moves from eternity to eternity according to the same principle. So in every age there exists a level of perfection but obviously not an absolute perfection that would conceivably halt the evolutionary process.

The problem with the followers of the former religions has been due to the belief that once their Faith reached the apex of its establishment it has achieved absolute perfection and therefore the process of continual evolution and transformation has ceased. But, absolute perfection can only exist in the world of God. In the contingent world perfection is perforce relative which means that the evolutionary process of religions will not stop since the unchanging principle governs the world of existence. This evolutionary process is only applicable to the world of creation for in the world of God which is created of absolute perfection, evolution has no meaning. The perfection that is referred to in this world is none other than human life; we consider the human being as the perfect creation of God and manifestation of His attributes. Of course the "Perfect Man" is the manifestation of God. Other human beings are not the same.

In a human being there exists a spiritual reality and because of this we consider him possessed of two dimensions. On the one hand, he is the manifestation of perfections and we recognize in him signs of divine perfections, and, on the other hand, he is a creature of the contingent world.

The light of God has touched man and because of this we never trivialize the human station by regarding a human as an animal. If we entertain misgivings in Darwin's theory, it is because we do not consider that the conclusions he arrives at based on his theory are accurate. In other words, we do not accept that since human life has an animal dimension, that a man is an animal and that no higher or divine principle exists in him. The damage that this theory has inflicted on human culture has led to the inference that whatever is applicable to an animal may, according to the theory, be applicable to humanity as a whole. Darwin may not have wished to go that far.

Accepting the general view of evolution it would follow that since an animal fights to survive, human beings must do the same; since an animal is free to exercise unencumbered sexual activity, man has to do the same; since sex in an animal is considered a physiological need and has strictly a physical dimension, therefore the same has to be applicable to human beings. Other conclusions can also be drawn from such a comparison. Those who in the name of science misuse its principles end up denigrating the station of human existence to that of the animal, in effect removing from him all responsibility and accountability except that which may be expected from an animal.

We do not regard humanity in this light. We do not consider a human being as only a physical being which can simply be defined as the evolved form of the animal. In that view all that is applicable to the animal becomes of necessity applicable to man. We do not define human life only in terms of matter and thus refrain from placing him within limits of scientific constraint. In other words, we are not compelled to say that all things are subject to the dictates of a cause or causes which invariably determine and produce certain effects. Materialists believe that as nature is devoid of free will, human history too is a tale of compulsion. Scientifically this lack of free will is referred to as "Determinism". We do not believe in determinism in man. Man can only be a natural mindless follower of material causes if he could be regarded solely in terms of his physical existence. However, that is not the case; man possesses a heavenly dimension which is free from all material limitations. Because of this heavenly dimension, which we call soul, he can exercise free will. This freedom of action does not apply to all things; in many aspects of life he is devoid of this power, however where he is confronted with moral issues he can exercise free will.

In a passage from the *Priceless Pearl* the Guardian is quoted as saying that one of the beliefs that has undermined human ethos, been a major cause of decline in civilization and has weakened the foundation of morality is the principle that every action may be excused and justified by a cause which necessitates compulsory compliance.[13]

---

[13] *The Priceless Pearl*, p. 375.

For example, an imaginary child seems to be inclined towards corruption. His actions are wicked and he is going astray. The experts come together to analyze the problem. The psychologist looks for the problem in the child's psyche. The sociologist seeks the problem in the influence of the society. Eventually they reach the conclusion that such and such issue is the root cause of the problem. The concept of the relative influence of environmental impact is undeniable; however, in this approach the "experts" go so far as to remove the ultimate responsibility from any one source, and thus no one really considers himself responsible for the problem of the child. On this basis if one is asked as to the cause of his misdeed, he can confidently answer that the environment dictated his actions, and therefore, in view of that influence, he is blameless; his excuse becomes: "I did not want to be bad and in fact I could have been good and yet under the said conditions I became bad."

The power of religion awakens the awareness of the faculty of "free will" and "responsibility" in the human mind.

The concept of the effect of various influences on human behavior has been manipulated to such an extent that man has been reduced to the level of a set of nuts and bolts of a machine which must necessarily act the same way as other machines with similar set of nuts and bolts and in so doing to have removed from him moral responsibility and made him the slave of "influences". The Guardian has said that one of the major problems that has damaged the moral and spiritual standing of human society is the propagation and dissemination of this principle which places the responsibility of all misdeeds upon external causes. We believe that man, even though affected by a variety of external forces, remains possessed of free will which makes him capable of choosing, and it is in that choosing that he can decide to become bad or good. He evaluates each alternative based on the value he attaches to things and situations and moves in a certain direction.

These values are defined for him by religion, and it is on that basis that things assume merit. He proceeds in a certain direction and sees himself free to continue or turn back because he feels responsibility for the choices he makes. When it comes to the operation of the divine will or the effect of other causes he has no responsibility. Divine will and the effect of natural forces continue to have an impact and in such cases "personal responsibility" has no meaning. However in cases where responsibility is felt, it is man himself who accepts this obligation. Whatever action an animal commits as part of his nature cannot be labeled "good" or "bad"; that same action would be considered "bad" if committed by a man. The man who confronts the same condition may wish to act as an animal but it is not possible for him to justify that action saying it is part of his nature, since he is by nature possessed of free will which forces him into making a conscious choice. If he were an animal the condition would not have been "bad" but since he has passed the limitation of the animal, in him the action is considered "bad".

Man is possessed of a divine element, and since the origin of that divinity, God, is a single essence, man too is predisposed towards unity; if he inclines towards differences, he will become remote from his divine component. It is because of this natural inclination that the unity of mankind is part of our beliefs. Man has a divine origin and because of this his genus is unique; his reality is unique, and whatever prompts him to separate himself from this uniqueness, devalues his spiritual existence and therefore is unworthy of his attention. All the causes of unity must be reinforced. The unity of humankind is considered a fundamental unity.[14]

One must reflect on this interpretation. Man's origin is unique; if his understanding and conviction impel him to consider himself connected to that origin, he must then recognize his uniqueness. Whatever diverts him away from unity and towards difference and

---

[14] *Má'dih-i-Ásmání* (*The Heavenly Sustenance;* untranslated), vol. 9, p. 90.

separateness is in conflict with the basis of his existence and is alien to his true nature. Therefore any such differences should be put aside and every effort should be expended to realize, in its entirety, this unity. When this concept of oneness is realized, the golden age of human civilization will emerge. It is towards that achievement that we are moving. It is for the establishment of that perfect heavenly paradise in this contingent world that we strive. The news of the establishment of the kingdom of God on earth is the tidings contained in the Bible; it is the same tidings which have come to us in Islam.[15] The world will be filled with justice; God's paradise as it exists in heaven will be inaugurated upon the earth; the unity of man becomes realized so that humanity will be able, in as far as this world of existence will allow, to become the mirror of the unity of God, all of which would ultimately constitute the final epoch in the first age of the dispensation of Bahá'u'lláh.

---

[15] Matthew 9:6 and Surah Zamr (39) of the Holy Qur'an.

2. The Station of Man

In the inanimate world, all things move towards extinction. All conditions are transitory. Instability and unreliability are the distinctive features of this world. The edifice of existence is based upon imperfection and stillness. All things are the result of the coming together of elements, and this coming together is an indication of needfulness. The soulless animal, too, is of this transitory sort. It rises from nothingness and unto it returns. It does not step beyond the narrow confines of nature; it does not emerge from the darkness of matter; it does not seek a way to the eternal realm.

In this midst, it is only man that has signs of the supernatural; upon him a beam of light from the eternal realm has shined; he does not regard himself as only the product of matter; he is attracted to a different realm; he is not the prisoner of nature; he extends his wings and soars; he extends his hand and opens doors; he seeks and finds; he builds and beautifies. In a word, in him there is a sign of God.

God saith: "O Son of Man: Veiled in my immemorial being and in the ancient eternity of my essence, I knew my love for thee; therefore I created thee, have engraved on thee My image and revealed to thee My beauty."[1]

---

[1] *Hidden Words of Bahá'u'lláh.*

And again He saith: "O Son of Being: thou art my lamp and my light is in thee. Get thou from it thy radiance and seek none other than Me. For I have created thee rich and have bountifully shed My favor upon Thee."[2]

And again He saith: "O Son of Man: Thou art my dominion and My dominion perisheth not, wherefore fearest thou thy perishing? Thou are my light and My light shall never be extinguished, why dost thou dread extinction?"[3]

And again He saith: "Thy heart is My home; sanctify it for My descent. Thy spirit is My place of revelation; cleanse it for My manifestation."[4]

And again He saith: "O Son of Man: Thy temple of being is My throne; cleanse it of all things, that there I may be established and there I may abide."[5]

And again He saith: "O Son of Man: Put thy hand in my bosom, that I may rise above thee, radiant and resplendent."[6]

And again He saith: "O Son of Man: Ascend unto My heaven, that thou mayest obtain the joy of reunion and from the chalice of imperishable glory quaff the peerless wine."[7]

What else could be said about man's station? God regards him as His own and summons him to Himself; considers him a sign of His glory; bestows upon him the power to create; and confers upon him a glimmer from the sun of His wisdom. God has knowledge of all things unseen, and He wishes for man to possess a share of that

---

[2] *Hidden Words of Bahá'u'lláh.*
[3] *Hidden Words of Bahá'u'lláh.*
[4] *Hidden Words of Bahá'u'lláh.*
[5] *Hidden Words of Bahá'u'lláh.*
[6] *Hidden Words of Bahá'u'lláh.*
[7] *Hidden Words of Bahá'u'lláh.*

knowledge, so that through the power of the intellect he may find his way to true knowledge and thus unravel mysteries.

He Himself is a creator, thus He gives man the power to create; He is wise, thus to man He grants wisdom so that he may discover the secrets of things. And that is why He openly tells us "...He has created him in His own image."[8] Since He created man in His own image, He could not consent that he should descend into misery, become attached to this material world, lower his head and look towards what is unworthy of him.

The Manifestation of the Cause of God is asked: "How should we behave in your presence?"; "What manner of courtesy should we observe before the glory of Your being?" The Supreme Pen responds: "When you enter this threshold neither bow nor bend your heads as it is not seemly for anyone to abase himself before another. Do not prostrate yourselves nor place your heads on the ground, nor should you kiss the feet since it is not fitting that man should place his face upon the earth for anyone except He Who is the unseen, the unknowable."[9]

Regard the love and compassion of the Creator! He does not wish for man to belittle himself or even lower his head before the glory of His Manifestation or place it upon the dust. He has wished to exalt him so! Is it fair that he should debase himself from such heights of nobility and surrender himself to the ever-changing fortunes of this transitory world?

Let us be clear. Man's greatness stems from his soul for it is the soul that is his channel to the eternal realm. The stronger is such a spiritual bond to the heavenly realm, the greater is man's nobility. Our glory is in this that we have in us a sign from the Unseen,

---

[8] Genesis 1:27.
[9] Full text of this verse appears in the book *Amr va khalq* (*Faith and Man*; untranslated), vol. 3, p. 429. See *Kitáb-i-Aqdas*, verse 34, p. 30.

otherwise we are lower than the dust, and nothingness is better than us; in the vast expanse of this universe, that utterly insignificant particle which is of no account will be none other than us.

Thus man's station is lofty if he looks to God and remains steadfast and firm in His Cause. And none is lower than he who looks to himself, for attachment to self reduces man to a blade of straw whereas looking to God places the heavens beneath his feet. It would be a pity if in his heart selfishness overtakes Godliness and debasement replaces loftiness. May God shelter us from such calamity.

3. Appearance of the Mystic Gems out of the Mine of Man

The purpose of the one true God, exalted be His glory, hath been to bring forth the Mystic Gems out of the mine of man-- they Who are the Dawning-Places of His Cause and the Repositories of the pearls of His knowledge; for God, Himself, glorified be He, is the Unseen, the One concealed and hidden from the eyes of men. . . .That the diverse communions of the earth, and the manifold systems of religious belief, should never be allowed to foster the feelings of animosity among men, is, in this Day, of the essence of the Faith of God and His Religion.[1]

—Bahá'u'lláh

Why did the Bahá'í Faith appear?

Why did the Sun of truth emerge from the East?

What was the purpose of its Author?

Where can we seek the answer to these questions?

What is better than to turn our gaze toward His own words?

He has on many occasions revealed the meaning of these words and at each occasion, adopting a different theme, has removed the veil from a corner of the mystery. And if we look closer we see that these

---

[1] From *Epistle to the Son of the Wolf*.

manifold melodies have issued from the same instrument, and as He begins, such a pleasant tune emanates from this instrument of the spirit, that once it reaches the ear of the soul, it opens a way for the heart to discover the mystery.

On one occasion He writes: "The one true God, exalted be His glory, hath come to bring forth the mystic Gems out of the mine of man." It is a brief statement, which requires volumes of explanation. In answer to the purpose of the Bahá'í Faith no better words than these can be found.

"The one true God, exalted be His glory hath come..." What significance did He intend for these words? Let us ask Him. There is no need to ask as He discerns without the asking and perceives without words; He has access to what transpires in the hearts. Unasked He answers: "...the Dawning Places of His Cause and the Repositories of the pearls of His knowledge" so that He may make it known that the "coming of God" is but the shining of the Sun of Truth from the dawning place of His Cause. God Himself remains forever unseen. He does not materialize, nor does He remove the veil concealing the mystery. Whatever appears in His name is a face that has been illumined by His light, a face whose light has illumined the world.

Why has He come?

"...To bring forth the Mystic Gems."

What therefore is intended by the word "Gem"? A Gem is something that is permanent, that does not experience decline or deterioration. It is a reality that does not change; it is the foundation of existence, the basis of life. Its opposite is "material" which is temporary and transient; it may be seen but not for long; it masks the Gem and hides it from eyes and makes only itself visible. It is like dust on a mirror, like clothes on a man. It is like a heap of debris on a treasure of precious stones. The mirror is invisible until the dust is washed off; the body may be found once the garment is removed; the treasure cannot be unearthed till the debris is pushed aside. What may be seen by the naked eye is material; yet on the far side of material what one can discern with the inner eye is the "Gem".

In appearance soil and rocks cover and thus conceal the precious stones; yet by the aid of wisdom a way to the hidden treasure may be found. In search of the Gems one should roll up his sleeves, gird up the loin of endeavor, and push aside the debris until the way to the treasure is found. Man's existence therefore is referred to as a mine in which Gems are concealed. What is this Gem? He says: "…gems are significances…" and with this He removes every ambiguity in the meaning of "Gem". This mystery in man's existence is hidden from view by heaps of dirt and debris. This dirt and debris are nothing but material impediments, physical attachments, and physical conditions which catch the eye and charm the senses; they deceive and mislead; they create the illusion that man is nothing but this physical body. Is it not true that when we regard ourselves, what we see at first glance is our physical body? He has come to rescue us from this deception, to tell us that He has with His own hands placed the Gems of spiritual truth in the mine of our existence. Place the material to one side so that the spiritual essence may emerge; wash away the dust so that the gleaming mirror may shine forth; push away the matter so that the meaning may appear. In the world of matter nothing is seen but conflict, change and disintegration: darkness and corruption are its essential features. If these could be stripped away, the Gem would be found: that unique Gem, that enduring reality, that unchanging and permanent beauty.

If man could find an entrance way to the mine of his own existence, he would discover unity with all its splendor and purity; he would find that reality with all its beauty and perfection and thereafter what had been the cause of disunity would fade away. What had been the sign of darkness is forgotten, and what had been the cause of corruption is no more. And in this way the luminous Gem of human reality or the essential unity of the humankind manifests itself. The religion of God, which has revealed this unique Gem, can no longer become the cause for enmity and hatred: it will not separate; it will not alienate. This is the reason for the appearance of the manifestation of God.

4. What is meant by "Spirit"?

The world of existence is divided into various natural categories, and the members of each category have in common certain features and effects, all of which have been equally endowed. It is this mutual possession of such qualities that places them in a single group and identifies them by a single designation. It is also due to this division that the three major orders of existence may be identified and distinguished from one another. They are:

1. Mineral kingdom – With such attributes as dimension and resistance

2. Vegetable Kingdom-- With such attributes as respiration, ingestion, growth and procreation,

3. Animal Kingdom-- With such attributes as sense and mobility

From the study of the various attributes of each category several conclusions may be drawn:

Firstly, the attributes of the members of each order although seemingly numerous and dissimilar are in fact inter-related and mutually essential. For example respiration, nourishment, growth and reproduction in the vegetable kingdom are so closely related that it would be impossible to imagine the existence of any one attribute without the existence of the others. By the same token the characteristics of sensation and motion in animals cannot be considered independent of each other. It is because of this relationship and connection that the collection of the attributes of any category may be considered as a single reality and therefore identified by a single designation. For instance if we say that the vegetable is one category of creation which is endowed with the power of ingestion and growth, we have not erred since by referring to these two traits, we have also embraced other qualities which are necessary derivatives of these attributes. By the same token in the animal kingdom, reference to the power of sense perception is sufficient to bring to mind the combination of other characteristics inherent in the animal.

Secondly, each of these orders or categories of existence, possesses, in addition to its distinguishing features the qualities of the categories that are below it but is devoid of those that distinguish the higher category. For example plants in addition to the traits of growth and reproduction also possess the solidity and resistance of the inanimate object and yet members of the vegetable kingdom are bereft of the qualities of the animal. The animal in turn possesses in addition to its own powers the qualities of the mineral and the vegetable whereas the mineral only possesses its own characteristics and none that belong to the higher levels of existence. Therefore in each succeeding level of existence signs that are indicative of evolution and distinction in the makeup of that level may be discerned.

Since logic requires that every effect should issue from a cause, the appearance of these new traits in each category of existence requires a primary cause and it is this mysterious motivator or prime mover that in the terminology of philosophers and the people of religious belief is referred to as "spirit".

Thus spirit may be defined as the prime cause of the manifestation of distinctive effects and attributes inherent in each category of existence. And since the appearance of such distinguishing features is undeniable, no doubt regarding their originating and essential cause can be entertained. Since these attributes are of necessity mutually related and can be considered as the effects of a single generating spirit, it can be said that each level of existence is endowed with a unique spirit. This uniqueness in turn makes each category distinct from the others and leads us to our belief in the following definition of the concept of spirit for each level of existence:

1. The mineral spirit is the source of the power of resistance.

2. The vegetable spirit is the source of the power of growth.

3. The animal spirit is the source of the power of sense perception.

From the above discussion it is clear that the acceptance of the existence of spirit in each classification of existence is due to the appearance of these evidences and effects. And since such evidences call for a cause, we simply assign the term "spirit" to that cause. Now we must consider the nature or essence of this primal cause.

The vegetable, in its material structure, is dissimilar and of a higher nature than the mineral. In other words the manner of the composition of the elements of its makeup is such that of and in itself it evinces effects and attributes which are different and superior to those of the mineral. We therefore maintain that the additional qualities possessed by the vegetable over the mineral are due to the change in the arrangement and constitution of its elemental make up. We consider the emergence of the resulting composition which exhibits the new characteristic to be a sufficient explanation as to the cause of the change. Therefore, the presumption of a possible non-material source or prime cause becomes unnecessary. It can be concluded that the vegetable spirit which is the power of growth is strictly of material origin.

4. What is meant by "Spirit"?

By the same token the animal in its physical make up and the unique composition of its elements demonstrate attributes and qualities that are patently different from those of the vegetable, Therefore we can say that the appearance of the evidences of the new attributes, absent in the vegetable, such as sense perception and mobility, are due to a special and progressive arrangement of its physical elements which is radically different from the elemental structure of the vegetable. In explaining these new attributes we see no justification in believing in a non-physical originating and motivating source and thus we hold that the animal spirit, which is the cause of the power of sense perception, originates from and is inherent in the physical and material nature of the animal.

However, once we attempt to apply these same arguments to the category of the human existence, certain questions arise:

Does the human being occupy a special and distinct category of existence which like the vegetable or the animal possesses certain particular qualities unique to that category? And does he possess in addition to the qualities of the lower ranks, attributes and powers that are uniquely his and clearly absent in the other creatures?

What is certain is this:

Firstly, man can discover the unknown. In other words, what to him was a mystery before, the ignorance of which could be considered a defect or limitation in his physical make up, can be discovered. The discovery improves his life and adds to his comfort and happiness. He maintains this gradual progress and makes of himself a man different from what he was before. Furthermore, he perceives no end to this process and sees in the future the continuing and never ending potential of discovery and change.

Moreover, he is able to transfer this knowledge and experience, gained through the phenomenon of discovery, to his children as well as to others and in this way help them along the road to higher levels of perfection. This cannot be said of animals or vegetables; in compliance to the dictates of their instincts they remain unchanged over the course of time. The most marvelous of the animals cannot, under its own power, discover what is unknown to it, and the most intelligent of its species fails to experience the learning process without human instruction.

Secondly, man dominates nature and transforms the conditions of his living environment such that they become more suitable to his needs. Thus, rather than submitting to the prevailing circumstances that govern his life, he alters the environment so that it may submit to his wishes. He is also capable of extending this dominance and power of transformation, without interruption, into the future.

Animals or minerals, on the other hand, are compelled to submit to the circumstances dictated by nature and use whatever nature has placed before them in its raw and, for them, unalterable state. The act of combining elements which could lead to the creation of fresh, previously unattainable attributes, is impossible for them. They cannot transform the parts into a whole with a view to enhance their dominance over others; they cannot store the memories of changes and discoveries in order to manipulate and reorganize them to produce opportunities for further discovery into the world of unknown. Animals and minerals remain patently impotent of the skills man can master.

Thirdly, the life of each member of the human race is not limited to himself, as man feels the need of association and togetherness with others; he breaks out of the individualistic mould within which he is seemingly created and sees others as part of a community to which he belongs. He seems to be driven to break every barrier to gain entry into the world outside of himself and establishes relationships and unity with those of his species who have remained separated from him through various physical restrictions.

4. What is meant by "Spirit"?

An animal, however, has a solitary life and is generally unaware of the members of its own species other than those which are instinctively related to it such as its small offspring prior to their growth and separation from the nest. Insects such as bees, machine-like, live among other bees without experiencing the novelty of overcoming the state of strangeness and fear of the unfamiliar.

Fourthly, man is never satisfied with what may limit his thoughts and is always looking to enlarge and universalize his ideas, arguments and assumptions into general statements and release them from the limitations of time and place. An animal, on the other hand, is a prisoner of time and place. For example, if a monkey tries to acquire an apple which is out of its reach, it may make use of a wooden stick placed before it to achieve its end, and it may appear as though it has discovered something that up to that point had been unknown to it. However this achievement ends at this point as the monkey will not be able to store in memory the results of the experience in order to make use of it in a similar future circumstance. When faced with food at a distance, it will not look for a wooden stick to replicate the earlier achievement. It is unable to develop a link between this experience and previous experiences in order to develop a general rule which it can then apply to all such future situations.

It is only man who can, with the powers of memory, intelligence and imagination, pull together the past, the present and the future in order to issue a universal judgment demonstrating the fruits of the unique power and creativity of his intellect.

Considering these special and distinctive evidences, it can be said that man is in a "special and distinctive" classification of existence, a distinction that separates him from the animal and vegetable kingdoms.

Thus can we say that the attributes and characteristics evinced by man are the result of the special composition or make up of the material elements of his physical being as we have seen in animals and vegetables?

What is certain is that there is no major or substantial difference between the physical construction of the body of man and animal. In other words, the same physical systems existing in animals, such as respiration, ingestion, reproduction, bone structure, circulation of blood and the nervous system are exactly and entirely replicated in man. This issue is affirmed by the fact that in cases where, due to ethical or legal grounds, the dissection of human cadaver for the purposes of medical instruction and training is not permissible, animal remains may be used which can, in comparison with its human counterpart provide valuable and generally accurate data. Such physical comparisons do not always distinguish man as the more perfect species since certain faculties of some animals, in terms of power and capacity, are more perfect than those of the human being.

Thus, since the differences that exist between the physical make up of animals and vegetables do not exist between man and animal, it is surmised that the unique attributes which distinguish man above animal cannot be the result of changes in the physical composition or make up. This realization leads us to the inescapable fact that these unique attributes of man do not originate from a material source and are clearly operational outside of man's physical dimension as no other explanation for the manifestation of these characteristics can be adduced.

This very special and non-physical origin or source that is the cause of the manifestation of these unique attributes in man is referred to as the "human spirit".

5. Relationship of Spirit to Body

Having explained the meaning of "spirit" or "soul" in part one of this presentation, the discussions that follow will consider a number of problems associated with this concept and will present, however briefly, the various attempts made at resolving them.

Firstly, it should be noted that the words "soul" and "spirit" referred to in this presentation are used interchangeably and therefore any possible distinction between the two concepts as held by some of the scholars are disregarded in order to diminish the possibility of any confusion that may arise from such duality of meaning.

One such problem under consideration is the manner or mode of the relationship that exists between soul and body:

There is no doubt that there exists a connection between soul and body. The conditions that affect the soul are readily detectable through the effects and signs that appear in the body. As anger rises in a man, blood rushes to his face, and as fright overtakes his soul, the face is drained of blood and grows pale. Pleasure and joy bring a smile to one's lips as eyes light up, the eyebrows relax and wrinkles of the forehead disappear. The thoughts we entertain and the actions we subsequently undertake find expression in the resulting movements of our body. The sudden awareness of the need to visit a sick friend is followed by the affirmation of that need by our thought process which in turn prompts us into action as we prepare to set out to visit that friend.

We think of a scientific problem with a view to find a solution for it. Suddenly our fingers begin to move as we pick up a pen and inscribe words that express our thoughts on paper. Our spirit contemplates the greatness of the world of creation and the power of the creator and suddenly wonder and fear overwhelm us. The evidences of these conditions are immediately reflected in the actions of the body. The physical manifestations are sometimes so severe that the body trembles, skin hairs stand on end and hands and feet lose their usual control.

If body and soul are two separate entities, how does this connection and association between them take place? The materialists consider this connection between psychic states and bodily movements as evidence of the correctness of their claim. They say that soul is not an immaterial thing, and spiritual conditions are simply the result of the movements within any of a number of bodily systems or the action and reaction between the various physical components that make up the body of man. Thought is the result of the interaction between the brain and the nervous system. In the words of the German philosopher, Voget, the relationship between thought and the brain is similar to the relationship between bile and the liver or between urine and the kidneys.

The evidences offered to prove this pronouncement follow: in animals, the more developed the central nervous system and the nerve centers, the more perfect are their spiritual activities. In other words, an animal with a more developed central nervous system possesses a more refined spiritual power. Furthermore, conditions, material or otherwise, that can sedate or dull the nerves or somehow damage the nervous system or produce impairment in the normal operation of the bodily glands would also sedate and diminish the effectiveness of that spiritual power. And if the brain is impaired, the thought process fails to function. In other words if a sedative is injected into the body, the spiritual activity ceases. As any drug that either stimulates or retards the functioning of the glands enters the body, its effect on the activities of the soul as well as the intellect is perceptible and pronounced. The medical procedures that are prescribed to treat the disorders of the glands and the nervous system alleviate the psychological infirmities. Materialists ask, "Is this not adequate evidence to support the theory that spiritual conditions are originated or motivated through physical or material causes, and that soul, as an independent and immaterial agent does not exist?"

Those who do not consider matter as "reality" of the world of existence respond by saying that the relationship between two things can not necessarily lead to the assumption that they are of the same origin. There are many existing material relationships that do not share the same origin. A dress hangs from a nail in the wall. If the nail becomes loose or drops to the floor the dress also drops; if the nail is sharp it may tear and damage the dress. Nevertheless, despite this relationship we cannot equate the dress with the nail.

Also a material entity and a spiritual entity can influence each other without belonging to the same classification of existence. A person's benevolence causes him to contribute some of his money to a needy individual without any assumption that the sense of charity and money are the same thing. Therefore, the fact that there is a relationship between the conditions of the body and those of the soul should not lead to the conclusion that body and soul are of the same make-up; it is possible that the two are of different natures, and yet there is a connection and attachment between them.

What is generally evident in the relationship between soul and body relates mostly to the states and conditions inherent in the animal spirit, which are those that are shared by both man and animal such as physical inclinations, emotions, deliberate movements and others.

The animal spirit, as discussed in part one of these presentations, is not apart from the body or its physical composition but, according to some scholars, is its consequence, result, or its ultimate expression. There is general agreement, in any case, that in the animal kingdom, soul and body are part of the same organic make up and that the two are not independent of each other.

However, the human spirit whose distinction and salient feature is the power of discovery of the unknown through the logical processes of the intellect is independent of the body and continues to endure after its passing. In man the spirit and body are not of the same origin as in many cases when a man's body becomes infirm and weakened and its power deteriorates, its intellectual activity remains intact and even in old age when man's bodily capabilities are impaired, the evidences of his wisdom and judgment appear more acute and intense. For example, one would think that after the age of forty when man's physical powers begin to decline, his mental capabilities and power of judgment should experience a proportional deterioration. Not only is that not the case, but, in fact, the opposite is true.

There are cases when physical and mental weaknesses may be simultaneous; however, since this usually is not the rule it cannot be concluded that the origin of both weaknesses is the same. In cases of physical limitation due to the effect of medication or to an injury sustained to the head in which the functioning of the brain is impaired, the lack of response may be attributed to an interruption of communication between the soul and the body. The body is an instrument for the manifestation of the effects of the soul; therefore, injury to this instrument has caused a disorder which has obstructed the appearance of the soul's effects in the body, not that the disorder has affected the soul.

Imagine a warrior who is exhibiting his power and courage through wielding his sword. If that sword breaks or its edge becomes dull, the display of his bravery becomes less evident or impossible. Such a situation cannot lead us to think that the origin of his sword and his courage are the same since if the warrior is given a proper sword, his valor will again shine as before. The same example may be applied to the relationship between the body and the soul. As soon as the bodily disorder is removed and a healthy brain is placed at the disposal of the mind, the same spiritual functions at the same level of perfection will be manifested.

Thus in accordance with the pronouncement of the "Spiritualists" the body is an instrument that acts according to the dictates of the spirit. The logical approach of the "Materialists" can only go so far and clearly falls short in proving that the nature of the soul and the body are the same.

Here the thought may occur that assuming that the body is an instrument for the soul, how does this manipulation take place? As manipulation of any instrument would require direct physical contact between the manipulator and the instrument, how then does such a contact between a non-material soul and the physical body occur?

Any assumption of the idea that the soul is something that enters the body or otherwise is in material contact with it is erroneous. It is this idea that has prompted the materialist surgeon to say that:" So long as my scalpel does not make contact with something called soul I will not believe in it", demonstrating the fact that the "human spirit" or the "rational soul" is an external entity in relation to the bodily frame. It has never entered the body or otherwise resided there. It has not been breathed into the physical body so that it may be manifested through a man's spoken words; if such references are found in religious or philosophic Writings, they have been used as symbols and metaphors rather than as expressions of reality.

Soul's origin is independent from that of the body, and its connection with the body may be explained as some sort of "attachment". Think of a mirror placed before sunlight. The rays of light are not detached from the sun in order to reside in the mirror but rather the sun's rays strike the mirror and are reflected to the outer world in accordance with the construction, location and condition of the mirror. At no stage of the process does the sun descend into or penetrate the mirror, and no unity between the two entities results.

In the same manner, the spiritual power, which flows freely across the world of existence and safeguards the universal order and is considered the origin and cause of the essential relationship between the realities of things, finds reflection in the human physical make-up. The intensity of such a reflection is dependent upon the degree of the spiritual sensitivity and capacity with which each human being is endowed. After that, spiritual power, in a sense, becomes localized and is attached to human individuals and assumes a specific and personal identity; in other words, it finds a sense of belonging to the physical being with which it has established such a connection.

Since that universal power is the protector of the order of the universe as well as the essential relationship between the realities of this world's component parts, its manifestation in each human being emerges as a power or bounty which not only concerns that individual with these essential relationships but makes of him a person who can discover such associations and be able to formulate them into universal laws and express them in clear and logical language. It is this power that has been called the human spirit or the rational soul and its chief characteristic is the discovery of the relationship between the reality of things and the establishment of their indiscernible unity in the face of their apparent diversity.

6. Proof of the Eternal Nature of the Spirit

One of the difficulties in discussing the concept of spirit is the bizarre and mysterious nature that is attached to the word by the common people. In other words the term "spirit" evokes an imaginary apparition such as a fairy, a genie, a ghoul or a demon in the minds, whereas the real meaning of the spirit should be amongst the most ordinary, familiar and intimate concepts for man. Once the true nature of spirit is properly explained, it becomes clear that such a term reflects neither the wonders of the supernatural worlds nor the legends and myths believed by the superstitious; the naïve associate spirit with such flights of imagination as communicating with the denizens of that "other" world through holding of séances or other similar deceptive practices.

Man's consideration and examination of the concept of spirit or soul originates in his reflection and study of his own being; that is as it should be since basically spirit or soul is really nothing but one's "self". From the moment that man turned his attention from the outside world towards the world within and began to examine what he saw or what he knew, he also wondered about the nature of the part of him that was actually doing the seeing and knowing, and thus his attention was drawn to the concept and significance of soul or spirit.

At first he considered the spirit to be of material and physical nature, and all early images and impressions of it are expressed in material forms. What remains to us of the ancients' impressions of physical objects is not much different from their concept of the "spirit" except that they held the spirit to be a more refined and delicate entity such as steam, smoke, air, fog, dust and other similar phenomena in nature. Since in the ancient legends, they believed in the survival of the soul after the death of the body and that its ascension to the heavens was a type of winged flight, they represented the soul as a bird or a fly or even a bee. The Greek philosophers of the fourth and fifth century B.C. made observations on the nature of spirit that must be considered the most original and profound elucidation of the concept and among the fairest fruits of human mind in the history of man's intellectual awakening.

Prior to this, spirit was considered as breath, which is exhaled by human beings. man, through the respiratory system, inhales and draws the spirit from the outside air into his being, and in this way spirit is generated within the human frame. It is due to this understanding that the designation with which the soul is identified is the word "breath" in both Greek and Hebrew.

In Arabic, spirit, connotes the concept of "breathing life into" the human body. In the holy Qur'án the same usage is adopted. In Surah 15, AL-HIJR, verse 29 it is recorded: "And when I have fashioned him and breathed into him of My spirit (spirit here stands for a vital force which imparts to man a participating energy with nature), bow before him in homage."[1] In verse 12 of 66th Surah, At-Tahrim it is recorded: "And of Mary, daughter of 'Imrán who guarded her chastity, so that We breathed into her a life from Us and she believed the words of her Lord and His Books, and was among the obedient." Note that even in divine revelation, the use of spirit is associated with the concept of "breathing into" the physical frame.

---

[1] Verse 29, Surah Hajar (15) and Verse:12, Surah Tahrim (66) of the Holy Qur'an.

This indicates that from the outset the explanation of a spiritual phenomenon appearing in a physical body had to be expressed in sensible and material terms comprehensible and imaginable by the believers and that the selected designation of such phenomenon had to have an appropriate association with the physical frame. That is why the representation of the phenomenon of spirit was in physical terms such as breath, air, steam and smoke and then, over time, gradually transformed and assumed a non-physical or spiritual quality. In other words, with the passage of time man began to realize that soul or spirit cannot be a physical phenomenon. Perhaps the oldest people, who understood the true meaning of this dimension of human existence, as taught to them by the word of God, was the Jewish people. In the Torah we note that soul or spirit begins to be expressed in spiritual or intangible terms. Furthermore, in Greek philosophy, in the works of Socrates and Plato, and after them in the Writings of Aristotle we note that the subject has been treated as a non-physical phenomenon. Plato, however, was the first to present the concept in definitively non-physical term.

Now, regardless of historical precedents, let us consider what really is intended by the term "spirit". It was noted above that the words "spirit" and "soul" were used to denote the same phenomenon, although at times, certain differences in meaning between the two may be implied. In such cases "soul" is regarded as the abbreviated form of the Rational Soul and is used to indicate the essence of a human being or the non-physical part of the human existence; whereas, the word "spirit" is utilized to indicate the life-creating force or origin of life that is shared by all grades of existence, e.g. the vegetable, animal and human life forms.

Sometimes also the reverse of this is the intention. In other words, when soul is used there is a connotation of the physical life, and spirit concerns itself with life after the death of the physical body. However, the two terms have been used interchangeably, and differences between the two have disappeared and presently signify the same concept.

What is then meant by "soul" or "spirit"? Spirit is the combination of qualities or attributes that distinguish the various grades of existence from each other. These grades or kingdoms share certain attributes, yet the combination of the characteristics that are unique to each grade and that distinguish it from the other kingdoms is called the "spirit" of that category of existence. Note that by the word "spirit" we are not referring to some strange, unintelligible or mystifying entity. For example in the vegetable kingdom, spirit or soul, is that original impulse which causes the appearance of the manifold qualities in plant life, such as growth. This attribute is an indicator of the existence of a special motive power that distinguishes the plant from the inanimate object. This motive power is called the "vegetable spirit".

In the same manner, what distinguishes the animal spirit from the vegetable spirit is the combination of those attributes that are absent in plant life such as sense perception: seeing, hearing, feeling, smelling and taste. This "animal spirit" shows that in the animal there exists an original principle that can cause the appearance of these distinguishing features that are absent in the vegetable kingdom.

In man, too, the soul or the spirit is nothing more than the same original motivator that produces those qualities that are unique to human life and that are clearly absent in the other grades of existence. By the same principle when we refer to the "soul" of something we really mean the "self" of that thing, and thus, when we refer to the "soul" of a human being we are referring to the actual "self" of that person: the soul of man is nothing more than his "self". Avicenna, in his *Ishárát* (Definitions and Counsels)[2] points to the

---

[2] *Alishárát va Altanbihát (Definitions and Counsels;* untranslated), vol. 2, pp. 319-325.

same concept where he says: when you say "I", or when I say "you" it is our souls that are speaking; therefore, the words "my soul" and "I" become interchangeable.

For example, in phrases such as "I went" or "I came" or "I saw" and even in those phrases in which the self is used as the object such as "I told myself" or "I reprimanded myself", we call the determining reality to which the verbs are applied "soul" or "spirit"; this is the same reality that exhibits the attributes, conditions and actions that are identified as "I" and which makes that "I" distinct from all other subjective realities.

Therefore the words "soul" or "spirit" should not evoke something strange, alien or astonishing. It is due to this point that when He sets out to offer proof of the nature and existence of the Spirit, 'Abdu'l-Bahá in *Some Answered Questions* presents arguments in support of man's distinctive attributes and merits.[3] In other words, the proof of the existence of man's soul is nothing but the expression and demonstration of those qualities and traits, which set him apart from other categories of existence. Therefore, 'Abdu'l-Bahá's method in proving the existence of the soul is to show that in the human species there exists a quality, an essence which belongs to him solely. So, human soul is nothing more than this distinguishing feature that makes him a uniquely separate and superior being.

Now we have to consider whether or not, there actually exists in the human species something that is conspicuously lacking in the animal. Of course on the face of it the issue seems to be clearly obvious since when we consider man, we see him as distinct and superior to the animal as we find in him qualities and traits that are patently absent in the animal. This matter is clear and obvious. What remains is for us to show that when we say "human spirit" or "human soul" we do not refer to anything other than these distinctive features. Once we

---

[3] See *Some Answered Questions*, pp. 200-204.

demonstrate this concept, the existence of "human spirit" is proven or at least has become undeniable.

Now what are these distinguishing features that only exist in the human species? One such feature is the power of thought. Man thinks and the animal does not. This is an idea than can be confidently put forward. The animal does not think. Of course the animal is possessed of intelligence; the higher category of animals such as chimps and various species of anthropomorphic monkeys possess intelligence of a practical nature and are capable of finding solutions for a difficulty that may confront them, but this is not the power of thought.

At its core, thinking is a deductive process, which is the capability that empowers man to devise practical solutions for any problem that confronts him. It enables man to discover both the nature of and solution to any problem once and for always. Moreover he possesses the capability to make such a solution universally applicable without the aid of any outside element or source and make of such a process a general and universal rule applicable in all similar cases. The generalization of discovered findings or solutions to problems, their accumulation and storage and their application to relevant future cases is the sole specialty of the human mind, and of which power the animal is completely bereft.

Of course modern psychologists who are more inclined towards materialist philosophy have attempted to show that the animal is capable of generalization of concepts. However, this has never been proven in practice. Man is capable of completing certain preparatory steps that would lead him to a conclusion. This conclusion is a new phenomenon that up to that point had been non-existent and therefore unknown to him. The discovery therefore increases his knowledge and becomes the basis for discovery of other unknowns thus revolutionizing his thoughts, his science, his industry, his life and himself. This phenomenon, that is, the changing of oneself through one's own ingenuity is specific to man; some scholars say that man is the only species that has a history.

When we say other species have no history, we do not mean that they are devoid of a past. Of course every creature, both individually and as a part of any given species has a past. In the course of time the creature goes through a process of modification and transformation the description of which could be regarded as its history. However, man's history is written by himself. In other words, man does not merely change but is the prime cause of that change. Unlike man, an animal is changed by the requirements and exigencies of nature or other external forces. Therefore, evolution in animals is a forced or compulsory process whereas in man such an evolution is deliberate, scientific and logical. It is the human species that can discover an unknown and in so doing change himself and become what he had not been before.[4]

You can witness the skill of the honeybee in the making of honey and depositing and storing it in the hive, and you may not see such wondrous talent in human beings. In fact, from among the most talented engineers, you can find none who could claim to be able to produce honey or construct a hive as brilliantly as the honeybee does. Obviously, human industry can never match bee's natural ability in this respect. However, the bee will continue to make its honey the same way it has always done, and its natural physical evolution over time cannot create any changes to the process either due to additional knowledge gained through discovery of any unknowns or results of any previous experimentation. Thus, the bee is unable to change, modify or enhance its art or utilize this marvelous talent in other areas and create something new or channel that ability towards an innovation or variety hitherto unknown.

---

[4] See *Some Answered Questions,* pp. 201-203.

6. Proof of the Eternal Nature of the Spirit

It is due to this power of thought that man's station emerges as distinct and sublime, and it is due to the existence of this wondrous quality that 'Abdu'l-Bahá places such great emphasis on this issue and affirms that man's distinction is credited to the power of discovery which flows from his thought processes. He explains that in plant life there exists the power of growth that defines its spirit, and the power of senses identifies the animal spirit. The power of discovery, however, specifically belongs to the human species; this power enables him to discover the unknown and in so doing arrive at a world he has not seen before. In this way man revolutionizes himself and what he owns, whereas the animal remains what he has always been and will continue to be.

Another distinctive characteristic of man, the existence of which none can doubt, is the power of consciousness. Consciousness refers to an intellectual capability that empowers man to experience all that he says, feels or does in a two- step process. Step one comprises the actual activity itself (the expression of an idea or an act), and the second step is the knowledge or awareness that accompanies that action or utterance. In other words, a man does not merely do something, he is also aware of what it is that he is doing. He does not just want something, he both wants something and is also cognizant of that state of desire. This power is that of intellect and consciousness.

Let's suppose you experience fear, an emotion that is also shared by the animal. The animal experiences fear but man's experience of that state of fear is unique, as he is also aware of the nature of that emotion. In other words, he has the power of understanding and consciousness that guides his every action. This phenomenon has also been called the "power of thought". Here of course the word "thought" is used in its general and universal sense. When Descartes said: "I think therefore I am" and considered thought as the best evidence of his existence, or the existence of his soul, he was referring to what we today call "intellect". Here the word "thought"

62

is being used in its widest sense and not as a process that starts as a premise and ends at a conclusion or traverses from a known and arrives at an unknown.

Man is endowed with the faculties of intellect and consciousness (and conscience) which accompany his every thought, act and condition and yet cannot be considered as having a physical source or be attached to man's physical existence. One can observe the effects of a non-physical condition in the human body. For example, when one experiences fear we recognize its immediate effects on the heart rate or the nervous system. And yet we can neither understand nor hope to discover the nature of that sense of awareness that accompanies the condition of fear.

A number of materialist psychologists have suggested that this state of awareness or "being conscious" is not a significant qualification of being human vs. being animal. They propose that this is not a phenomenon but an epiphenomenon that emerges as a secondary or attendant phenomenon. To understand the concept of epiphenomenon, the following examples are relevant. When we light a match, the friction of the matchstick against the rough surface of the matchbox serves to ignite the flame. Friction then is the cause and flame, the effect. In this example friction and flame are both the primary and principal phenomena while, say the reflection of the flame on a nearby wall is considered an epiphenomenon as such an appearance had not been intended and falls outside the natural and essential purpose of the exercise. The power of steam propels the locomotive that moves the train. The principal cause and effect here are the generating power of steam and the movement of the locomotive respectively. However, there also appears an attendant phenomenon, say the sound that is generated by the movement of the cars. Secondary phenomena or epiphenomena are phenomena that do not belong to the principle or intrinsic cause and effect process but are created as subordinate, attendant and inherent phenomena.

The materialist psychologists claim that the same applies to the intellectual process. They suggest that the "cause" is the external stimulant or motivator and the "effect" is the condition that appears in us; therefore, the sense of awareness or consciousness that accompanies such perception is simply a secondary phenomenon that has no influence on the main cause/effect process.

Of course, such a conclusion is faulty, and even those who had proposed the theory themselves have since admitted its fallacy; awareness of an act does, in fact, affect the condition of our response. The anger that is accompanied by awareness, understanding and consciousness is quite unlike the same emotion that has a mere physical and animalistic manifestation. Understanding and consciousness are possessed by man alone; the existence of these conditions are beyond and outside of the normal processes and functions of the human body, which man shares with the animal.

Another distinctive characteristic of man, that is specific to him, is the concept of free will. Animal action, whatever it may be, is the effect resulting from a cause or causes outside of itself. This means that we cannot say the animal took an action as it willed to do so and that it could have done otherwise had it chosen to act differently. In man however we can say that John could have acted differently but did not or he could have acted in a certain way but he chose not to. Thus, there exists in man the power of will that allows him to choose according to its dictates. First he experiences doubt and upon study he chooses an approach and commits himself to it in action. Having thus made the choice, he becomes responsible for that selection and has to abide by its results. Since he becomes responsible for deciding the choice, he may experience a pang of regret if the choice turns out to be wrong, or feel a sense of fulfillment or satisfaction if the choice proves to be right. This process only exists in man. In an animal this power is absent, and thus the animal cannot say I chose to do such and so whereas I could have done otherwise.

6. Proof of the Eternal Nature of the Spirit

The existence of the power of will in man is undeniable; not only does he sense that power but he is also aware that all the actions he takes are within his power to avoid. This leaves no doubt as to the existence of will power in man. Now once we admit that we are capable of taking action according to our own will, we have no choice but to accept that we are distinct from the animal and that in us there resides a non-physical or non-material phenomenon which is the source of this controlling power. This is true because there is no quantitative or qualitative correspondence or correlation between "Matter" and "Free Will" since everything material obeys the rule of cause and effect and follows a pre-determined course of action. However the rule obviously does not apply here.

The materialists consider "Matter" as the primary substance of human life and deny the existence of a non-material and non-physical soul. They consider man as a purely physical being and reject the existence of will power. Therefore if we dispute and disprove the concept of "determinism" we will have shaken the very foundation of materialist beliefs.

The materialists are quite emphatic about this issue since it is in the rejection of the existence of the will power in man that they can make of him a mere material creation and thus deny him the possession of a non-material spirit. They claim that whatever happens in the mineral, the vegetable and animal kingdoms is the result of external cause or causes and that nothing takes place due to the exercise of an independent will power. Similarly, they consider the same to be true in man. They wish to demonstrate that no human action can be the result of free choice and maintain that the claim to will power is at best a superficial theory and even the seemingly freely-willed actions have dormant causes or grounds which drive man, unwittingly, to pre-destined consequences. These causes or grounds may be inherited, absorbed or due to the effects of the prevailing environment.

6. Proof of the Eternal Nature of the Spirit

The materialists go so far as to consider the effect of heredity as having its origin in environmental causes and thus they consider the biological effects of heredity in man to be subservient to environmental influences. If this theory is accepted, materialism finds a foothold on the basis of which everything would have to be measured by the "material" scale. This would then lead to the notion that when man takes a particular action and claims personal will as its cause, he is simply in error since external causes are and must be the real initiators of any action and that man is simply ignorant or unaware of these external causes. Thus actions that are claimed to have been taken as a result of choice will be defined as material and natural in their origin, forces of which, man is ignorant. Because of this ignorance man has the illusion that his will is the motivating agency of the action. This claim is put forward as a scientific theory since, in the materialist's vernacular, the word "scientific" implies or relates to the "material" and the "physical" worlds and nothing more.

Note that this idea is one that has simply been adopted but not supported by observation and experience; we can only call a theory or idea "scientific" if it can be so justified. Interestingly in this case observation supports the opposite argument which is corroborated by the dictate of one's conscience. As an example, one can say: "My action was initiated by myself through the exercise of choice, and I don't find myself ignorant in any way. I say that I committed a certain act through the operation of my will and I can support this claim by having experienced indecision and doubt at the outset as to whether I should or should not go through with it; this uncertainty demonstrates that the selected choice is the result of the exercise of my free will."

To make everything material and physical all actions have to be made subject to the principle of cause and effect and subordinate to outside forces and environmental influences; were that so, it would make willful action an absurd and irrelevant claim. So while I clearly feel absolute freedom in the choice of my action, I am being invited by the materialist to admit to an error in my judgment. In most cases the material philosopher simply denies the obvious just so that he can prove the point he has adopted. Note that the word "adopted", is used since this verb demonstrates his freedom to choose an idea and embrace all its implications even though these may be in conflict with the results of observation. There are of course great philosophers such as Kant, Bergson and Heidegger who believe in the existence of the power of will in man. They approach the issue differently and, having evaluated the results of observation, are led to accept man's freedom to choose.

Therefore, we conclude that the existence of free will, which is one of man's salient characteristics, cannot be denied. Once such a conclusion is arrived at, man automatically places himself beyond the limits of the material, since the realm of material is the realm of constraint and coercion; in so doing he proves the existence of a non-material motivating power within him. The "spirit" of man is nothing but this very power. This is something that is only specific to man, something that is not material and physical. That is what we had intended to demonstrate. We wished to define "spirit" as a special source or matrix from which all human qualities and characteristics flow. This source or origin cannot be material, since if it were then these qualifications that issue from it: thought, conscience, free will, etc., have to be categorized as physical attributes which clearly they are not.

Once the existence of human spirit is thus proven (by "proven" we mean "undeniable" since the concept of man's spirit is not a subject that can lend itself to scientific proof as do physical concepts) or that we cannot deny its existence; its eternal nature is also undeniable. Spirit is accepted as a non-physical and non-material concept; therefore, the idea of its extinction as a result of the death of the body is no longer tenable. That which dies with the death of the body must necessarily be of a substance identical to that of the body or issued from the body or be of a physical nature. When, as

67

described, this is not the case, and spirit is seen as an origin or source from which non-physical qualities are derived, that source itself also cannot be physical. We must therefore submit that we cannot accept the proposition that the destruction of the body will extinguish the light of the spirit since what dies with the body are elements that are of the same nature as the body. This line of reasoning not only supports the concept of the existence of human spirit but also proves its eternal nature. Once the non-physical nature of the spirit is established, its eternal nature follows as a matter of logic. Thus it should be clear that the demise of matter does not and cannot cause the extinction of spirit.

7. Questions and Answers Regarding the Spirit

1. When does the spirit abandon this world?

The spirit, which we consider abstract, placeless, and immortal, is neither an animal nor a vegetable spirit. What infuses life into vegetable and animal is a material condition and the result of the composition of various physical elements. There is no connection between this and the eternal human spirit. The life that is the result of the commingling of material components is, as 'Abdu'l-Bahá puts it, "... like the light from a lamp that is the result of coming together of the wick, fuel and a lighted match. Once this convergence is disengaged the light will also be extinguished."[1]

The human spirit is the source of Intellect, Love and Will. Destruction of the body or more accurately the decline of the physical body in its ability to reflect its light causes the spirit to discontinue the manifestation of its qualities through that body.

'Abdu'l-Bahá in His presentation of proof for the existence of the spirit considers sleep allegorically. He states that:".... spirit is non-material, since if it were not then in the state of sleep when body's

---

[1] *Some Answered Questions,* "Soul, Spirit and the Mind," pp. 208-209.

physical powers are at rest, no activity should be detected whereas in that state we are distinctly active."[2]

The point made is that what appears to us in a dream reflects the movements and activities of those bodily faculties which are, in reality, in repose and suspension during the course of sleep. It is this phenomenon that evidences the connection between the spirit and the world of sleep.

What does this mean?

How does one see? First the eye must be open so that light may enter and form an image of the subject on the retina; this image must, in turn, be transferred to the brain through the optic nerves so that the subject may be identified and understood. If these conditions are not met, in other words, if there is no subject before one's eyes or the eyes are closed, then the image of that subject cannot be perceived through the faculty of sight. Even if the subject itself is absent and is merely being remembered, this is not considered an activity of the faculty of sight since one clearly accepts and admits that the brain is not seeing but only remembering. For example, you recall the face of your brother while he is absent. How do you consider this condition? You are clearly aware that your brother is not actually before your eyes. Whereas, in the world of dream something quite tangible appears before you that causes you to be completely convinced of its reality. This is entirely different from the experience of wakeful remembering that is accompanied by the understanding that the subject is in fact non-existent at that moment.

The act of seeing is dependent upon the continuous functioning of the faculty of sight. If this faculty is inactive and dormant during sleep and if one could still be convinced of the reality of what he is seeing in the dream state, it becomes necessary to

---

[2] *Some Answered Questions*, "The immortality of the Spirit," pp. 227-229.

conclude that one's spirit without the active participation of any of its bodily faculties can bring into the realm of existence things that are, in fact, non-existent. Thus, it become clear that there exists within each human being a mysterious engine which is capable, without the participation of man's bodily faculties, of producing, in a special and inscrutable manner, such actions as are expected only to appear from these physical faculties in the state of wakefulness. The connection of sleep and the spirit exists, therefore, to this extent.

None of the existing classifications of created beings are at a level to have multiple spirits. In other words, the concept of multiplicity of spirits in any one being is devoid of truth; it is impossible. It is not possible that an animal be endowed, separately and in addition to its animal spirit, with the vegetable spirit. The possibility of two spirits in any one being is unrealistic and contrary to reason. It is as if matter takes on two different appearances, i.e. a statue appears as a dog and a human being at the same time. At any given time matter can only appear in one shape.

A human does not have three spirits. To assume separate vegetable, animal and human spirits in a man is opposed to logic. For each class or category of existence there exists only one spirit; however, that spirit can also reflect the powers of the spirits of the lower classes of existence. For instance, the animal spirit in the animal also possesses the powers of the vegetable spirit; however, although it is endowed with both sets of powers, they appear within a single spirit that reflects both qualities. The proof of this point is that the characteristics of the lower grade of existence appear differently in the higher level. For example, the vegetable's process of injection, respiration and growth appears differently in the animal. In other words these functions are influenced by the animal's powers of sense and mobility, which cause the manifestation of these functions to appear differently.

The physical powers of the human being, too, are influenced by the human intellect and thus appear differently than those in the animals. The animal instincts that exist in man emerge under the control and within the limitations imposed by the human mind and manifest themselves in a different manner and at a higher and more refined state.

In reality, each higher power or higher level of spirit attracts and absorbs the powers of the lower spirits and manifests them. However, the manifestation of the combination of such powers originates from a single spirit. This is applicable to all grades of existence including man's spirit and the Holy Spirit, which appears in the human form and transforms the bearer into a manifestation of God.

While he is on earth and in order for the soul to manage the needs of the physical body, which requires the powers of the vegetable and animal spirits, the human spirit creates and manifests such powers within itself without being in need of animal and vegetable spirits. (The same is true for an animal when compared to a vegetable.) However, after the death of the human body, nothing of the vegetable and animal powers remains; all of these powers are lost as they are of no further utility. After death man becomes eternal through his human spirit.

The concept of advancement or regression of the soul from a lower category of existence to a higher one or vice versa is false. Neither is possible. For example the animal spirit can never elevate to the level of that of the human; the human spirit is an independently unique creation with a sense of belonging to the human body. A creature that is not so endowed can never hope to advance or evolve to such a profound spiritual state. Thus it would be impossible for an animal to become human.

This concept is in line with Darwin's theory of evolution of species. In other words, if we say man was at one time an animal and then evolved into man, it does not necessarily follow that any animal that possesses an animal existence can develop and be transformed into a human being. By the same token, a man cannot achieve the spiritual qualifications and rank of the Holy Spirit. In other words an ordinary man cannot achieve the spiritual level of prophethood. The spiritual ranks are inviolable. This inviolability applies both to the elevation and regression of spirit. The human spirit can never retrograde to that of the animal unless the conditions for the full manifestation of its qualities are not made available. The emergence of the human spirit is a unique phenomenon and its manifestation is also a singular marvel.

For example, a mirror is placed before the sun; if the mercury that is used in its construction is defective, or if dust has covered its surface or if an object has blocked the sun's rays from reaching it, then the light of the sun cannot be reflected. But this does not mean that the mirror is devoid of the potential to reflect light. Only man is endowed with the human spirit, and yet if physical impediments impair the proper functioning of the body, man's human characteristics fail to become wholly reflected, and his life inclines toward its animal dimension. This does not imply that the human spirit has abandoned him but that due to various obstacles the manifestation of his spiritual characteristics has become impaired.

It would be impossible, therefore, for the human spirit to lower itself to the level of the animal and by the same token the animal spirit can in no wise elevate itself to that of the human. However, the spirit of the higher plane encompasses that of the lower plane without the reverse being true. This means that man is aware of the conditions of the animal and can guide, control and train it. While this does not mean that man can become animal, it does mean that he has the ability to dominate and control the animal. By the same token the Holy Spirit has supremacy over the human spirit. On the other hand, the human spirit after its release from the body rises to a higher dimension of existence and thus can dominate the lower spiritual levels.

This does not mean that this control is of a type we can comprehend in this material world. In other words, one cannot claim that his father's spirit can actually see him since the act of seeing as we know it has no meaning for him. Seeing is a characteristic of this body. Seeing requires light, color, the physical eye and a specialized system of nerves and therefore in the spiritual dimension such an act of "seeing" is meaningless. By the same token if one claims that his departed father can hear his voice, he has expressed an unrealistic concept since the departed spirit has no physical ear that can enable it to hear. The sound that is perceived by the physical ear has no existence in the world of spirit. \Since spiritual perception, spiritual emotion and spiritual domination take place within the spiritual dimension they are of a totally different nature than similar qualities that are comprehensible to man in the physical realm; of the comprehension of that nature and condition, we, as physical beings, will remain forever incapable.

Why is it that man is incapable of understanding those spiritual qualities? Because he is not at a level of existence where such an understanding may be possible. While in the mother's womb, the fetus has no conception of his future conditions; however, now through scientific discovery we are cognizant of the condition of the fetus, a condition which is outside its own ability to understand. The human spirit can comprehend and have knowledge of the conditions of the material world through spiritual perception and power that can only have meaning and application in that sphere of spiritual existence and of which we remain totally ignorant. Such a spiritual knowledge is not derived from the powers of sight, hearing and other sense perception capabilities with which physical bodies are endowed.

The materialists consider "Matter" as the matrix of all that exists. They claim that since the spirit has no outward or material manifestation, and since it is not tangible, cannot be seen by the naked eye and cannot be perceived by any of the senses, it cannot exist. If we say that intellect, knowledge, free will, selfless love and the like exist (none of which lends itself to physical sense perception), materialists respond that these are the results of the proper functioning of the various components of the human body and are, therefore, basically of material origin.

So why does matter exist? Because it is tangible! And yet if the proposition is that whatever that is beyond sense perception does not exist, interestingly enough matter itself also falls in that category and should be considered non-existent. Why? Because what we see of matter is its color, what we feel is its temperature, what we hear is its sound, what we taste is its taste, none of which can be considered matter as these are the attributes and qualities of matter and not "matter" itself. These qualities can be perceived by the senses without matter itself exhibiting such capability.

So the "matter" of the materialists does not lend itself to sense perception. It can neither be seen since color gives it its visibility, nor heard since sound gives it its audibility, nor is it tangible since pressure, heat, and texture give it its palpability. These are manifestation of the characteristics and qualities of matter, which are perceptible. Matter, that is the essence and origin of these attributes, is not.

The assumption that what is intangible is non-existent, therefore, also disqualifies matter as an existing phenomenon since its tangibility cannot be demonstrated. It is with reference to this very point that 'Abdu'l-Bahá has said:

"The very essence of nature is an intellectual reality.[3] We do not discover the nature of matter through sense perception but through intellectual reasoning." In other words, any attribute must have a source, bear a trait and appear within a context: evince temperature, color or sound. That necessity leads us to the understanding of the existence of matter. Therefore, we arrive at the intellectual belief in something that is intangible by the logical manipulation of tangible traits or characteristics. It makes no difference whether you believe in matter or in spirit since in both cases we arrive at the realization of an intangible phenomenon through intellectual assessment of tangible attributes.

The error of the materialists is in this very point that matter is tangible. Whereas, what is tangible is not matter but its attributes, its qualities, and its characteristics. Matter itself is not tangible. What we perceive through the senses is not matter but its attributes. It is from these qualities and supported by the universal principle of cause and effect that we arrive at the existence of matter.

Thus if the existence of any intangible phenomenon is to be denied, then first we must deny matter itself and like Phenomenologists profess belief in color, sound, temperature, pressure and alike without understanding the source of their existence or where and in what context they may appear. This is in conflict with logic and is also not supported by the materialist's view.

In fact, the intellectual proof of the existence of an intangible matter, that is based on recognition of a source for every phenomenon or a cause for every effect, is no different than the approach by which the existence of an intangible spirit and an intangible God may be demonstrated.

Nature and matter are not tangible phenomena, but intellectual realities. What we see of these in the tangible world are their

---

[3] *Some Answered Questions,* "The Five Aspects of Spirit," pp. 143-145.

qualities. They are attributes of that intellectual source and as such, whether matter or spirit, have no outward or physical form and are not located in a particular "place". A "place" only recognizes outward qualities. Matter is intangible and placeless.

Thus, if a thing can exist and though intangible yet be the source of tangible phenomena, any hesitation in the acceptance of the existence of spirit as the intangible source of physical manifestations of our emotions and conscience would be unjustifiable.

We believe in the connection between body and soul. A living body has a distinct relationship with its spirit. This relationship is that of the manipulator to the instrument being manipulated. A soldier wields his sword and demonstrates his courage; the carpenter's handiworks are produced through the use of the saw; however, the soldier is different from the sword though his bravery is manifested through the use of the sword; the carpenter is different from the saw though his skill is exhibited by its use. If there were no saw, the carpenter would still have his intellect, his industry and his skill albeit the manifestation of this intellect, industry and skill would not be possible.

The connection between body and soul is the relationship between the instrument and its manipulator. Man, through the use of the instrument of his physical existence must channel his spiritual energy and power into action. If this physical instrument is non-existent, the spiritual power cannot be manifested although it continues to exist. A deformed mirror reflects distorted images although the image itself is in perfect form. If someone's brain is damaged, his thought process is disrupted his mind itself remains unaffected. Thus, the brain may become damaged, but the mind or the power of intellect remains unaffected although it is through the use of the brain that it manifests its power. Therefore, a damaged brain may produce confused and deranged thoughts.

When blood flows out of the body what comes to an end is the manifestation of the power of the spirit through the body not that the spirit has been destroyed. Take away a soldier's gun from him; he is no longer a warrior in the field of battle. Not because he no longer exists or that he is unable to manifest his courage but that the instrument, through the use of which he could make war and showcase his bravery, is not available to him.

The connection of the realm of spirit with the physical world, or as a whole, the world of creation with the Kingdom of God is through the kingdom of Divine Will or through the Manifestation of His command. The spirit is also the handiwork of God and part of the world of creation albeit not in itself a physical creation. After bodily death the connection between human spirit and God is through the kingdom of Divine Manifestation, or more accurately, the Divine Manifestation Himself; no human spirit can ever have a direct connection to the essence or the "self" of the Divine. God is beyond the knowledge and understanding of man; he has been and shall remain forever in a state of utter unity and absolute invisible mystery. When the human spirit separates from the constraints of the physical body and is released from its connection to the world of matter, its connection to the Divine Manifestation becomes stronger; the human spirit after the separation from the body acquires a closer relationship with the Holy Spirit than it had in the physical world.

8. Non-involvement in Political Affairs

One of my Bahá'í friends gave the principle of non-involvement in political affairs a most imaginative title; he called it "the Talisman Principle" which suggests that the principle serves as a sort of amulet for the protection of the friends as well as for the Cause of God. An amulet is an invocation, a supplication or a prayer that is either recited or is inscribed and worn as an armband in order to protect the bearer from harm. He had called this principle an amulet since it has always been a safeguard for the protection and safety of the Faith and of the friends. His wit and flair in choosing such a title is undeniable.

Politics is defined here as the management and administration of the affairs of a country. Involvement in such management and administration (aimed at leading a country towards a desired ideal) is what the people of Bahá, in accordance with the teachings of 'Abdu'l-Bahá', the beloved Guardian and the Universal House of Justice, shun. They consider any involvement in such activities outside the sphere of their religious beliefs and spiritual commitments.

It is essential that we explain and elucidate this principle and this commitment to both the friends who, in accordance with Bahá'u'lláh's teachings, have become accustomed to assess the truth of every issue through the agency of their own intellect before submitting to it, as well as to non-Bahá'ís who may wonder as to the logic of such a belief.

We know that the fundamental Bahá'í teachings have a moral, spiritual and ethical character. In other words, the purpose of the Bahá'í revelation has been to perfect the life of the spirit, extol the spiritual realities, enhance manners and morals, and reinforce the power of conscience. Bahá'u'lláh states that the aim of the Bahá'í Faith is the reformation of humanity, the advancement of the world, and the elevation of humankind. All of the tenets, teachings and principles which He espoused are based on this foundation so that the world, through strengthening of morals, ennoblement of human conscience and exaltation of ethical virtues may advance to such heights of greatness. Any approach to achieving these goals other than the Bahá'í Faith, is considered temporary, unsuitable, or unreliable.

In other words, we are confident that unless man receives spiritual education and training, hearkens to the call of the spirit, and ultimately achieves his highest spiritual potential, he will not find true happiness. Any and all other efforts to reach such a goal, while not necessarily detrimental, will only have a temporary, superficial, and tranquilizing effect. Furthermore, such other approaches would only focus on the material aspects of the situation and, thus, not offer a complete, accurate, and reliable solution. Concentrating only on the material aspects, therefore, would make it impossible to construct a vibrant, strong, contented, forbearing and free society when the individuals involved may be morally ambivalent, ethically unstable, spiritually bankrupt and emotionally uncaring. Piety emerges as the mighty pillar of Bahá'í life because the focus and the actions of the people of Bahá concentrate on the spiritual, ethical and moral aspects of humankind.

Before all else an individual Bahá'í must be pious, must have belief in God, must be God loving and God fearing. This fear stems from love: fear of God for a Bahá'í may be likened to the fear of a lover at committing an act that would break his beloved's heart. It is in this manner that we say that a Bahá'í should fear God, which means he must be pious, and his piety is more important to him than anything else. Without it, nothing else in the world would matter. What is important for us is piety, the sustaining of piety and the strengthening of piety. Therefore, any factor which may prove to be in conflict with a chaste and holy life is shunned by a Bahá'í, and whatever that may assist in its strengthening and reinforcement is embraced by him.

Should a day come when the entire population of the world or of any nation become Bahá'ís and yet they fail to adhere to the principle of a chaste and holy life, not only have we not succeeded in our duty but in effect we have pushed that world or that nation backward and have achieved exactly the opposite of what we had intended to achieve. Piety is our main goal.

There is an expression that says: Piety ends where "politics" begins. We have no choice but to lay politics aside so that we may be able to safeguard our piety. Lack of piety does not constitute a disadvantage for the world of "politics". In fact lack of such a religious principle in politics not only has no detrimental effect, it may very well be the cause of a politician's success.

Before I explain further, let me quote you a saying from Ali, (son in law of Prophet Muhammad). The Arabs faulted Ali for not being a politician. They claimed that he lacked the acumen, the shrewdness and cunning that are the necessary tools of a statesman and asserted that because of this he was incapable of adopting the necessary expedients to defeat his rivals. Ali heard this complaint and replied: "If piety did not exist, I would have been the best of statesmen." He meant that it is not that he was ignorant and incapable, but as he wished to safeguard his righteousness, remain a just and honest man, and be true to his Faith, he stayed clear of politics.

Clearly this issue is not unique to the people of Bahá; it is a general religious principle and a matter of conscience. Whenever the leaders of religions wished to emphasize the safeguarding of piety, they have advised that whatever method politics requires in order for it to succeed is incompatible with the requirements of a pious life.

Success in politics is a critical requirement, and in order to succeed, one must compete with opponents or adversaries. It is not possible for one to enter politics without having to deal with opponents. In such competition for power bargains must be struck; compromise and conspiracy come into play; empty promises are made; lies and half-truths become routine declarations, and publicity stunts, chaos and commotions abound, If we choose to abstain from adopting these methods, we will be defeated as our opponents will not pull any punches.

What, then, is the purpose of involvement in such politics where, if we try to remain faithful to our beliefs, we have to accept defeat? And yet if we decide to entrap and overpower our opponents, stab adversaries in the back, lie and sensationalize in order to succeed, then we have abandoned piety and nothing is left of our devotion and obligation to a spiritual and ethical life. In effect, participation in politics, in so far as our spiritual life is concerned, degrades and demeans us. If our spiritual and ethical beliefs are thus undermined, nothing would be left of our Bahá'í life.

Politicians have an axiom which says: "The end justifies the means." In other words, it implies that we should adopt any available means, regardless of their nature, in order to realize the desired end. The idea is that since a good end is of principal importance, adoption of even bad means which will guide us to that good end is acceptable and justifiable. Every politician has no choice but to accept this attitude since if he rejects it, he will not experience the glory of victory. If a politician becomes unwilling to consider all available means and from among such options chooses the one which is in line with moral principles, he will experience the pain of defeat; his opponents will have no qualms in seizing the opportunity to embrace the most effective means regardless of their ethical value. Obviously, should one persist in adhering to his principles and continue to accept defeat, he will no longer be a participant in politics. However, if he does choose to participate and adopts whatever means necessary to achieve the end which he considers as good and desirable, soon finds that this end has become tainted and distorted. Those who have accepted corruption as a means cannot ultimately achieve a good end. A good end, once in the hands of a corrupt individual, will become tarnished and discredited.

In order to reach a good end which is in line with the principles of the Faith, a Bahá'í does not resort to bribery. He will not bribe someone so that he may serve the Faith. Why? Because while he considers the goal as good, the mere act of bribery has despoiled that goodness, and, thus, what is there that remains of the Bahá'í Faith which he may wish to serve? Since the basic belief in the Faith is piety, then our aim is piety, and such devotion to a righteous life becomes inconsistent with any participation in political affairs.

Another issue to consider is the involvement in political affairs by an individual who wishes to take it upon himself to advance a certain political agenda. Such a situation, in our current world, is not viable. Participation in politics requires belonging to an established party that has a defined constitution with particular attitudes and beliefs. If a Bahá'í chooses to belong to a particular party: Democratic Party, Socialist party, Communist party, Republican Party, etc., he must of necessity adopt their principles and beliefs, some of which may be in contrast with such concepts as God, the hereafter, purpose of life, etc. By joining a party a Bahá'í on the one hand must adhere to the principles of the Bahá'í teachings and consider them as true, and on the other must accept the basic tenets of a political party and regard them as true. It is obvious that these two belief systems cannot be compatible. If a Bahá'í accepts a party in which he believes all aspects are in line with the Bahá'í ideals, he has not abandoned his Faith, has not joined a different party. However, should he decide to belong to this other party, he has, in effect, dissociated himself from the Bahá'í Faith.

The Bahá'í Faith is itself a party and has been referred to by Bahá'u'lláh and 'Abdu'l-Bahá' as the "Party of God" (the term has since been adopted by other political entities which bear no relationship or resemblance with the Bahá'í Faith-Translator). The members of the "Bahá'í party" in whichever country they may reside will be obedient to the governments of those countries. The "Party of God" is a party with its own spiritual and moral teachings, among which is, for the present time, avoidance of involvement in political affairs. So anyone who is a member of this party is a member of the Bahá'í community. A Bahá'í may see no difference between simultaneously belonging to the Bahá'í Faith and a political party as compared to being a Bahá'í and an atheist at the same time; or an individual who is both a Muslim and a Buddhist; or a Muslim who may also be a Christian. Thus, while one cannot confess to belief in all these religions as each is an independent Faith (unless we regard their fundamental principles which is a different discussion) by the same token an individual cannot be a Bahá'í and belong to any political entity.

This of course does not imply that the people of Bahá' should not be educated in the organization and management of world affairs, the correct approach in serving one's country, guidance and service to the people, and the duties of government officials. Such a disregard of current world affairs could imply that the Bahá'í Faith is an isolationist and socially disconnected organization. On the contrary, the Bahá'í Faith offers progressive economic and social teachings, and although expressing belief in a spiritual world, it has principles that govern the mode of operation of these social teachings. The Bahá'í Faith differs from political entities in that it does not adopt political means to achieve its avowed fundamental goal, the unity of the human race.

There have been a number of social ideologies that have adopted a worldview in their principles and policies and have focused on the unity of humankind. And yet as they entered the arena of political enterprise they were confronted with competing ideologies which they had to defeat in order to advance their cause. The results gained from this approach were completely contrary to their envisioned aim and thus eventually they reverted to the practice of imperialism and exploitation: goals which they had intended to avoid. This underscores the fact that should adopted means be incompatible with the intended end, the means will eventually undermine the end and render it ineffective and unproductive.

The Bahá'í Faith does not wish to follow this path. What this Faith intends is to bring love to hearts, create friendship between individuals, encourage and strengthen ethical conscientiousness, refine morality and expand the spiritual teachings among all people. The achievement of these goals will supply the building blocks necessary to build the fortress of human happiness confidently and firmly. should one who wishes to build a magnificent structure but instead uses substandard and shoddy materials that are incompatible with the design of the building, then such a project is destined to fail and such a structure is obviously doomed to destruction. Even if the building reaches its completed state, it will eventually collapse.

A Cause which has as its goals the unity of the human family, promotion of love and affection among people, and the exaltation of moral values surely cannot afford devotees who may be corrupted by worldly competition, bargains to achieve a certain goal, and plots and intrigues to gain a political aim. In such a case, the structure that Cause is raising and the goal it is working toward will never be realized, and ultimately it will join the other ideologies which have failed to achieve the end they had originally envisioned.

An inquiry was sent to the Bahá'í World Center asking the following question: "How should world political affairs be regarded by the friends? Political issues are unavoidable. Therefore, in what light should participation in world political affairs be seen?" The Bahá'í World Center referred the friends to the relevant writing of the beloved Guardian elucidating Bahá'u'lláh's teachings regarding this issue. The Guardian writes that there are two simultaneous processes taking place in the world: one is the natural and imperceptible yet essential evolution and the other is the deliberate and steadfast organization and teaching activities that are performed by the friends in the path of service to humanity. The purpose of the world Bahá'í community is the diffusion of the teachings of Bahá'u'lláh in order to achieve the goal of the unity of the human race. On the other hand, another process that is natural and innate and is based on the essential relationship between the realities of things is also moving forward. In other words, the world and all that is in it is, by the force of nature, moving towards a destination, of which the people of Bahá' are well aware and in which they believe. The aims of these two processes are the same except that one moves naturally and the other deliberately through the teaching efforts of the Bahá'í community. In the first process, political affairs, naturally and essentially, find a role to play and do so without any impetus. On the other hand, the people of Bahá exclude politics in their efforts to teach the Cause of Bahá'u'lláh. The meaning of non-involvement in politics is this: we who teach Bahá'í principles make every effort to bring hearts and souls together, strive to expand the cause of world unity in accordance with Bahá'í teachings, and do not include political methodologies in our approach. Since our individual lives are focused on service to community life, if we are corrupted we will have weakened the efforts that are put forward by the community to reach its goal. We must put aside any thought of participation in political affairs in our individual lives so that we may remain safeguarded from the moral breakdown that would threaten the sacred and holy lives to which we have dedicated ourselves.

Let us now pass from our theoretical discussion and consider the effects of such actions which highlight the benefits of non-involvement in politics for the Bahá'í community and the Faith itself. The Bahá'í friends in this hundred and thirty five years (now over hundred and sixty nine years-Trans.) have passed through much adversity and experienced many ups and downs in their individual lives. If they were to involve themselves in political affairs, join various parties and ideologies which have emerged in this period, and actively participate in the realization of their goals, today no sign of the Bahá'í Faith would remain. Why? Because each would have gone his own way and along with his fellow ideological comrades would have trodden the path of decline and eventual extinction. This would have caused such diversity of thoughts that even if a group which identified itself as Bahá'í were to endure, it would remain as a sect, a faction or a cult of which history can give many examples. All that would remain could be seen in a name and a feeling of unwitting attachment. The independent nature of the Faith, the true devotion of its adherents, its organization, teachings and goals would have passed from memory.

Consider the emergence of the Faith in its opening stages. After the proclamation of Bahá'u'lláh, a group of Bábís rejected him and became violators of the covenant of the Báb. The followers of Azal (known as Bábís or Azalís) subsequently became active in political affairs and over time disappeared from history; today those individuals who still belong to such persuasions usually hide their identity so that they are not seen by their countrymen as different in belief and thought from the rest of the nation. This was a good experience as a lesson learned; involvement in politics was their death knell as a religious community. Obviously, there is no reason to think that had the Bahá'í friends followed the same path they would not have arrived at the same ending.

In this period there emerged many ideologies and political sects. Since most of the friends were educated and capable, they could have easily joined these groups and become active in advancing their noble agendas. Yet results of these various agendas would have resulted in the complete breakdown of Bahá'í community life as each group would have been in conflict with the others, which ultimately would have led to their downfall and extinction. Could one have imagined then a day, like today, when we have Local Spiritual Assemblies in the far corners of the globe or Bahá'í centers in thousands of locations around the world?

Those who oppose us have always waited patiently to find a political justification in order to accuse the friends of wrongdoing. This is because they were unable to denounce them for any faults due to their religious beliefs as these beliefs were openly known to all and none of such principles conflicted with any divinely ordained laws. It is astonishing that, on the one hand, they degrade the friends for not participating in political activities and, on the other hand, accuse the community of meddling in political affairs and classify the Faith as a political organization in its core.

One is at a loss whether to laugh or cry at this illogical conundrum. What is crystal clear to us and to others, and agreed upon by all, is that we do not participate in political activities. What those who oppose the Faith have is an empty accusation and at no time, in these hundred and thirty five years (now 166 years-translator), have they ever been able to present a document which could serve as evidence to show our involvement in politics. Of course, it is possible that an individual Bahá'í may have had some participation in politics or given his consent to achieve a political end. However, the Bahá'í community has always separated itself from such individuals so that the community may remain protected.

If our opponents found any actual evidence of our involvement in politics, then you would have witnessed ordeals descending upon the friends. How many times have they put a stop to our administrative activities? How often have they closed the doors of our Bahá'í properties? In all these cases, they seized the premises, searched every nook and cranny and never found an iota of evidence. Had they found any such indication, then you would have seen a litany of charges the friends would have been accused of.

Thus, non-involvement in politics has been our true amulet.

In fact, during the Persian constitutional revolution, 'Abdu'l-Bahá's strict instructions regarding non-involvement of the friends in the political upheaval not only safeguarded the believers (otherwise it was not clear what would have happened to the friends and the Faith itself) but also, as stated by a Bahá'í scholar, preserved the Iranian constitution. Why? Because the opponents of the constitutional government could not find an excuse to accuse the Bahá'ís of being the main thrust of the constitutionalists and proclaim them as unbelievers in Islam and thus infidels. This was a mystery which helped the natural evolutionary process of events that led to the establishment of the constitutional government and also protected the friends and the Cause through the deliberate guidance of 'Abdu'l-Bahá.

In one of his Writings, the Guardian tells a relevant story. Some years ago the friends were accused by the authorities of a neighboring country of belonging to a mystical religious sect which was banned in that country. The friends were formally accused, their activities investigated, their papers and Bahá'í Centers confiscated, and all the papers kept in Bahá'í centers and those of the Local Spiritual Assemblies were examined. The beloved Guardian asked us to consider what would have happened to the Bahá'í community and the Faith itself had the authorities found any shred of evidence, written or otherwise, of the involvement of the believers in politics.

The very reference that the Guardian makes to this particular event sets an example for us. It is a lesson for us to remember and keep in mind that regardless of the time and place of our residence, the nature of issues, or the conditions under which we live, we leave all participation in and management of all political affairs to those who are not Bahá'ís, and if they ask why we abstain, our answer is clear. What we do is to transform hearts, refine conduct and strengthen our ethical and moral behavior. Whether this policy and approach is essential to our well-being; whether it is appropriate or not; or whether it is of benefit or not, for us its suitability is clear.[1]

Others won't take on the responsibility for the edification of the human family, and we have assumed this responsibility. Others, then, can assume the political duties. The matter is very clear. If the spiritual duty of the safeguarding of moral uprightness and rectitude of conduct by bringing together the hearts and souls of members of the human family estranged from each other is essential and beneficial, then it is only fitting that those who have focused all their attention on such a service should be freed to carry on their work, and others should take up the work from which Bahá'ís abstain.

Tempting baits are set for the young Bahá'ís in order to attract, entice and encourage them to involve themselves in political affairs. However, Bahá'í youth are aware, attentive and vigilant. They know

---

[1] In *Directives From the Guardian,* p. 87, the following guidance is given for all Bahá'ís: "The friends may vote, if they can do it, without identifying themselves with one party or another. To enter the arena of party politics is surely detrimental to the best interests of the Faith and will harm the Cause. It remains for the individuals to so use their right to vote as to keep aloof from party politics, and always bear in mind that they are voting on the merits of the individual, rather than because he belongs to one party or another. The matter must be made perfectly clear to the individuals, who will be left free to exercise their discretion and judgment. But if a certain person does enter into party politics and labors for the ascendency of one party over another, and continues to do it against the expressed appeals and warnings of the Assembly, then the Assembly has the right to refuse him the right to vote in Bahá'í elections."

that in such activities, the words that flow from the tongue are different from the purpose that is hidden in the heart. Usually the politicians argue that: "How can one be so apathetic to the destiny of his homeland and still claim to be a patriot?" In other words, if one loves his country, how can he remain uncaring of its destiny?

The answer is very clear. We are not uncaring of the destiny of our country. We do not excuse ourselves from working for our homeland. We accept, with heart and mind, educational tasks that are among the most critical requirements of any country. We consider activities related to the economical growth of the country important, and we participate in them with honesty and uprightness. Any activities that lead to the development and progress of the nation we consider to be acts of service and do not shun performance of them. The attempt to acquire wealth, in accordance with applicable laws and full payment of associated taxes to the government, is in accordance with the tenets of the Bahá'í Faith. And although the Bahá'í Faith is the religion of peace, yet in the times of war, people of Bahá accept to be drafted into the armed forces in accordance with the laws of the land. However, they prefer to be listed as noncombatant personnel who should not be required to be placed in the front line of attack where killing would be inevitable. However, in all other services they will fully participate.

Therefore, who can say a Bahá'í is apathetic about the destiny of his homeland?

The Universal House of Justice has said that the friends should not assume that the principle of non-involvement in the political affairs of their country provides any justification for them to remain aloof from working for the welfare and wellbeing of their fellow countrymen and in so doing remain idle and fruitless. Rendering service does not have to be only through politics. If service is meant to be rendered strictly through the medium of politics, a

Bahá'í will not take up such a service. But you must admit that the road to service does not necessarily have to go through politics. This political service with its associated requirements of ambition satisfying a sense of self-glorification and earning assorted benefits and privileges, we freely leave up to others. Let those services that require self-sacrifice, detachment, the giving of oneself, hard work, and the earning of an honest and honorable living be our lot. We do a good job at this and we should.

Bahá'ís do not disregard the interest of their country. Especially in the case of Iran, it must be said that the Bahá'ís, albeit unaccredited and unacknowledged, are the leading promoters of Iran, its culture, its race, its name, its traditions, and its interests in the world. People of this land love Iran as their homeland, but the Bahá'ís have a certain distinction for they revere Iran as the birthplace of the Bahá'í Faith, as the place of sacrifice of Bahá'í martyrs, as the soil in which the blood of the most loved members of the Faith flowed, as the soil which was made crimson with the blood of the Báb, the soil that was sanctified with the steps of Bahá'u'lláh. We are speaking of sacredness and not of mere devotion, of worship and not just love; we are speaking of the act of prostrating and placing of one's forehead on the ground; we are talking of diffusion of this love around the world. Today for hundreds of different races and nations and tribes across the globe, for millions of souls in tens of countries and in thousands of cities and villages, the name of Iran, the culture of Iran, the tradition of Iran, Shiraz and Tehran of Iran is revered and idolized.

They are not few, who from across the globe come to Iran so that they can place their foreheads on the soil of Shiraz where the Báb arose and in Tabriz, to shed a tear, where His blood stained the earth. And yet this pilgrimage that has been the goal of their lives, so that they may come and kiss the face of Iran and return, come to worship Shiraz and glorify Tehran and take a handful of soil of Tabriz in remembrance, if this is considered not appropriate by people or government, then such a pilgrimage will not take place since not only are the friends acting in accordance with their own principles but also they are accepting and obeying the decision of their people or government. Thus, how can such a group of people be considered apathetic towards the destiny of their country or be regarded as uncaring of rendering service to their homeland? This act of pure tyranny has been inflicted on the people of Bahá throughout the history of the Faith.

Another concept the politicians use to lure the young people into their trap is to insist that involvement in politics is the road to the establishment of justice in the world; therefore, how can a group of people remain uninterested in such a profound objective? Of course we know that this is only the mere appearance of the issue. Involvement in politics is simply the replacement of one class in place of another, one individual in place of another, one position in place of another, etc. When there is a political contest, the stated goal is to combat the ongoing avarice and self-indulgence of the system, but if we look closely we see that the election has provided the opportunity for the same self indulgence, wealth and rank for the other candidate who, not having possessed such benefits and privileges before, pined for the opportunity to possess them. The friends, who stay aloof, simply do not choose to be the instrument of the candidates or their ladder to success.

The people of Bahá know well that serving the cause of justice is only possible through service to the cause of humanity, achievement of the unity of the human family, establishment of world peace, abandonment of all forms of prejudice, strengthening of the power of conscience and awakening of the hearts to spiritual realities. Justice cannot be established in the world in any other way. We are not pessimistic or cynical regarding other human activities and aspirations; we consider these as part and parcel of the same natural movement or development that is essential, deliberate and inherent in the world of existence which must of necessity lead the world to that same ultimate and cardinal goal.

We do not focus our efforts in that direction. We work towards spreading the teachings of the Bahá'í Faith; we focus on expanding the influence of Bahá'u'lláh's principles, which are nothing but unity of the human family, improvement of the morals of nations and elevation of this contingent world to a level that may reflect the virtues and attributes of the Abhá Kingdom. We employ these instruments to reach our goal; we keep ourselves and our goal unalloyed, unpolluted and uncorrupted even if realization of such a goal may be in the distant future. This is because the goal that we strive to achieve is not a personal goal; it is a struggle so that the human race may reach its true destiny, a destiny which we may or may not get to witness. What is certain is that for this purpose we don't back down and will not compromise our principles in order to take any shortcuts. We will not try to reach our objective in haste and in so doing undermine its pristine quality, nor will we compromise the very purpose of Bahá'u'lláh's revelation due to our deficiency of understanding.

Our involvement in politics, in effect, would make of the Faith what we strive to prevent. Because of this not only will we not participate but we pray that the people of Bahá will stand firm against any involvement in political activities. This non-involvement has always served as safeguard and protection of the people of Bahá.

9. Heaven and Hell

I was asked by the National Committee for Distribution of Bahá'í Literature (Publishing Trust) to say a few words on the subject of heaven and hell as viewed by philosophers. This, of course, is not an easy task since these concepts are basically religious in nature and not philosophical and, as such, are not relevant to the field of philosophy. A philosopher will not speak on this subject from the viewpoint of philosophy since it is outside his scope. This is true unless the philosopher is also a religious scholar. Such an individual is referred to as a Doctor of Divinity in Christianity or a scholar of the science of the "Word" in Islam.

What do we mean by the "Science of the Word" in Islam or "Science of Divinity" in Christianity? The purpose of such a science is to offer proof of religious principles through intellectual methods. In other words, these scholars first adopt certain basic principles that are neither in conflict with tenets of divine revelation nor with the divine commandments. Then utilizing a rational approach and a logical methodology they derive relevant conclusions to demonstrate the conformity of such precepts to those religious beliefs, and through such an approach they establish the fact that there is no conflict between the pronouncements of religion and the intellectual requirements of logical proof. Such people cannot rightfully be regarded as "philosophers" in their true sense. A philosopher is defined as one who considers the dictates of the intellect and intuition as the only credible and reliable sources of knowledge. The philosopher's actions are guided by a logical process or intuitive knowledge and free from all influences of religious teachings, and yet such philosophers have no apprehensions if the conclusions they arrive at are consistent with any religious principle. In fact they freely admit of such agreement since they consider both pronouncements to be true no conflict could be expected.

However, while engaged in rational exposition, it is not the philosopher's intent to prove the principles of religion. These are philosophers in the specialized sense of the word, and, as such, they refrain from considering concepts related to heaven or hell in their discourse. Of course, they do explore the eternal nature of the human soul. IF they are believers in the Divine, they do present proofs in support of the principle, and if they are not believers they either offer evidences to the contrary or consider the matter to fall outside the realm of philosophy and state the issue does not lend itself to rational investigation and judgment. These philosophers become agnostics and make no attempt at either proving or disproving the eternal nature of the soul.[1] Thus concepts of heaven and hell remain outside of the realm of philosophy. They are studied solely within the arena of theological sciences despite the fact that these sciences are not without their connection with philosophy; in the Middle Ages religion dominated all aspects of life in both the East and the West leaving no philosopher free to express his thought without due regard to the principles of theology.

Avicenna tried his hand at such freedom and mostly succeeded. He made every effort to keep from entering the arena of religion and presented his views based only on intellectual interpretation. Yet he did not always succeed in doing so. One of his most curious

---

[1] Agnosticism is the school of disbelief in the power of the mind in understanding of reality and emphasizes the fact that perception of the realities of things fall outside of the capability of the human intellect.

pronouncements was his view of eternal life and the concept of resurrection. With regards to the nature of the human soul, he proved that the human spirit is eternal and that this enduring quality is a spiritual phenomenon. When he studied the concept of physical resurrection, he considered it to be a religious principle and added that his acceptance of the phenomenon was basically due to his religious devotion; the concept is clearly set forth in the Qur'án. Yet he admitted that the mind is incapable of proving this issue.

Thus, he considered spiritual resurrection provable by the dictates of reason, whereas physical resurrection falls outside of the realm of intellectual investigation, and he who accepts it does so based on his religious conviction. A few hundred years after Avicenna another philosopher named Mulla Sadra-i-Shirazi,[2] who, not wishing to limit his understanding of such issues, expanded his philosophical outlook and became involved in religious philosophy. He made an attempt to present logical proofs in support of various religious doctrines, specifically of the concept of physical resurrection. Whether he succeeded is another story.

Another discussion current in Eastern philosophy is the concept of heaven and hell. By "Eastern", we include the philosophies of India, China and even ancient Persia. The difference between Western and Eastern philosophy is that in these countries philosophy has never existed independent of religion. It would be impossible to write the history of Indian philosophy without also discussing Indian religions; religious beliefs are a combination of spiritual principles and philosophical ideas.

---

[2] To study the philosophy of Mullá Sadrá, refer to two sources that have been translated, summarized and published by Javád Muslih based on Mullá Sadrá's book *My Journeys*: (a) *Knowledge of Self* (or *Psychology of Sadr*, University of Tehran, 1974), (b) *Philosophy of the Higher Dimension* (or *Wisdom of Sadr*, Tehran University, 1975).

Some Greek philosophers have considered the issue of heaven and hell, and some have not. Those who have entered this arena haven't done so from an intellectual and logical viewpoint. They have done so based on their consideration of various mythologies current among them. For example, Plato, when speaking of hell refers to a subterranean world and even makes mention of geographical features such as rivers, creeks, mountains and springs, not unlike similar references in religious texts which speak to us of various levels of hell, wells, rivers, scorpions, snakes, and hell's blazing fires, etc. These are mythological discussions, stories, and allegories, and whenever Plato enters such philosophical discourse, he promptly interjects a mythical story into the debate so that he can exit the realm of logic and instead conjure up in visual imagery the purpose of his argument.

Aristotle differs from other philosophers of the time by generally abstaining from storytelling, saying nothing of heaven and hell and withholding any views regarding the eternal nature of the soul of man. In fact his reference to the issue is so vague that it lends itself to multiple interpretations. He refrains from any direct discourse on the subject of heaven and hell, and if he offers any ideas which may be so interpreted, it is only due to the accepted religious or mythological doctrines current among people at the time.

It is better, therefore, to classify the various philosophies and evaluate them in the light of a Bahá'í viewpoint. Since our discussion is religious in nature we must consider beliefs of ancient religions with regards to everlasting life and heaven and hell. To do this a preliminary review of the philosophical aspects of these issues becomes necessary.

The first group consists of natural or material philosophers who disbelieve in the idea of an invisible and non-physical entity called the human soul and hold no belief or recognition of the existence of God. Their world is limited to the world of nature, which makes any consideration of the concepts of heaven and hell irrelevant. As they have no belief in the human soul, the idea of reward and punishment in a non-existent world does not enter into the realm of their philosophy.

There are other philosophers who may be considered spiritualists or idealists who do not consider human existence as only a physical phenomenon. They believe in man's eternality and therefore their views regarding the nature of his soul are different from the material philosophers. Some of these spiritualists believe in the eternal nature of the physical body. Such a principle obviously originates in religious belief as such concepts do exist in religious texts. If these concepts are not considered as symbolic or otherwise interpreted as spiritual realities, the philosopher who proclaims continual existence of the physical body after death, expresses such a view no longer as a proponent of philosophy but of religious Faith. The views of such an individual are influenced by his religious convictions whether or not he is aware of that influence. If he is a Muslim, he will have one view and if Christian another view and if a Buddhist, yet another. The attempt of the spiritualist philosopher will be to present and prove religious principles as supported by philosophical or intellectual reasoning.

Some philosophers who believe in physical resurrection are proponents of metempsychosis or transmigration of spirit from one person to another. This belief is quite prevalent in India and other Eastern countries. The concept also existed in Greece and since Plato, the greatest of Greek philosophers, held to such a belief it is likely that others among the Greek scholars also supported the theory.

Those who advocate this concept believe that the pursuit of perfection for the human soul cannot be completed within the limits of one human lifetime. As one shirt is obviously not adequate for a lifetime of use, and one would wear out many shirts before the end of this physical journey, similarly the body is like the garment for the soul which once outworn is discarded, and the soul adopts other bodies until the road to perfection is completed.

As it transmigrates, man's soul in this physical existence becomes defiled and overly attached to materialism, loses its spiritual power, its freedom and its ability to soar away from this physical prison of self and realize the promised reunion with the ultimate reality. Because of this attachment to materialism, the soul has to endure its association with its physical existence until it reaches the desired goal; it puts on a physical garment, and when outworn, discards it in favor of another one. Which body does it adopt? That depends upon the level of perfection it has achieved with the previous body. Depending on the success of this maturing process the soul may have to reincarnate itself in physical entities that may be in a lower grade of existence than its previous body: an inanimate object, a vegetable, an animal or another human of a lesser level of perfection. Thus, the soul will continue its journey from body to body until it reaches the goal of its desire.

This belief is called metempsychosis or reincarnation, where clearly heaven and hell exist in this physical world. In other words, as the soul moves from one body to another, the new entity plays the role of heaven or hell depending on the acquired virtues or the shortcomings of his previous existence. When a man questions why he has been the subject of so much pain and agony in his life, he can consider his former existences and wonder as to the sins he must have committed then to merit his present misery. Once these transmigrations end and the physical body is no more, nothing remains of heaven and hell as the soul, unhindered by physical limitation, has completed its journey, reaches the realm of absolute nothingness and, in utter contentment, becomes one with Nirvana.

Philosophers do not accept such a concept, as the intellectual proof of this theory is very difficult; it remains a religious belief and nothing more. There are ample reasons to disprove the concept. If we hold to the belief that there is nothing beyond the physical existence, as materialists do, then the idea of a soul migrating from one body to another loses its meaning altogether. However, if we do believe in something beyond this physical existence, then that "something" is either common or specific. In other words, either this spirit is a universal entity whose relationship with all individuals is the same; in which case, such a spirit cannot be specific to any one person that would distinguish him from other individuals. However, if the spirit is considered to be specific, then it implies that such a spirit can only be attached to a body, which will reflect its particular characteristics. To reconstruct the "shirt" example given above, we must note that not all individuals can wear the same shirt. The shirt may be too tight or too large or in any case may not fit properly for all who try it. Each person chooses his shirts in accordance with his own taste and penchant. Although the example does not prove the case, nevertheless if we extend the example, it leads us to the conclusion that the relationship between a body and soul are specific and that such a soul cannot in fact leave one body and become attached to another.

Furthermore, this process entails a retrogressive migration that is contrary to the rule of nature as well as of God. Man's development is always in the direction of growth and maturity and not towards deficiency and defect. That man should experience a reversal in this process as he migrates from one body to the next and takes on the face of a monster that he had already discarded in his journey to perfection is illogical and untenable and has been rejected by philosophers and scholars alike.

Other religious scholars believe in a different manifestation of physical resurrection. They claim that after the departure of the soul from the body, it will not transmigrate to another body but rather returns to its own physical existence so that the body that has committed the sin may also receive the chastisement due to him in the day of resurrection. These religionists also believe in physical resurrection. They contend that from the time it leaves the body until the time of the end when it returns to that body, the soul continues in a waiting mode in some purgatorial state until the day of resurrection; at that point the body is revived so that the soul may return to it. The soul in its original body enters a world where his punishment or reward awaits him.

Of course, the religious fundamentalists who believe in the physical interpretation of scripture say that the body, in its normal form and condition arises, is resuscitated and prepares itself for the Day of Judgment. These religionists make no attempt to provide a logical basis for such a belief since they disregard the opinions of philosophers altogether. This has not kept such philosophers from taking up the issue and presenting a plethora of arguments in rejection of the concept of resurrection, finding flaws and ridiculing such theories by asking such questions as: which body is to arise? The one in its childhood, in his youth or his old age, which? In which state of health or its lack and at which time and day in the life of the body is it to be resurrected, since from birth to death the body goes through continuous transformation, and in the process some of its component parts may be removed and some added and possibly others may have been detached and added to other bodies. Considering the fact that the body deteriorates, disintegrates and becomes subject to complete decay, no return, reappearance or physical recurrence is logically possible.

Christian religious scholars, not unlike some of the Muslim clergy, in the Middle Ages believed that when the spirit leaves the body it is always ready to return to it, not the particular body it has abandoned but any human temple through which it can animate the same identity. Thus, the concepts of physical heaven and hell can find meaning and become applicable to physical resurrection, where the body, according to his deeds, can receive his due reward or punishment.

The people of Bahá do not agree with the concept of physical resurrection; they believe in the eternality of the soul and its resurrection. They consider such eternality as a spiritual phenomenon which is completely devoid of any association with the physical body. As to the state and conditions of the soul no opinion can be put forward; man, as a physical creation, falls within a category of life that is different in nature and essence from the world of the spirit and thus is utterly incapable of comprehending and unraveling the mysteries of that realm of reality. Bahá'ís simply accept the belief as one that is in line with reason and make no claim to any degree of understanding of that level of reality and its conditions; whatever thought or impression that is put forward must, of necessity, originate from and be comparable to elements and conditions existing in this physical world, leading to conclusions that are obviously unsupportable.

Hell and heaven have been interpreted in physical terms: heaven with its green gardens and running brooks, trees, milk and honey, apples and pomegranates or whatever that seemed pleasing and delectable to the people of that age and hell with its snakes, scorpions, fire and whip or any other chastisement that seemed horrifying to that culture. Obviously such a concept can only stem from religious belief as no intellectual or logical evidence can be put forward as its proof.

Philosophers on the other hand, regardless of religious belief, interpret the concepts of heaven and hell on an intellectual basis. They propose that since what remains from man, after his death, is his "Rational Soul", which possesses the source of man's intellectual power (or the mind), it follows that the soul follows a path dictated by the mind and as the mind is of the same origin and category as the "first mind" emanated from God, therefore the pleasure and happiness derived from heaven cannot be a sensual phenomenon but an intellectual one. On the one hand, this puts the philosopher whose realm of activity is the exercise of the intellect, in its strictest sense, in a favorable position. On the other hand, this is not the case in this plane of material existence since we are surrounded by the influences of physical phenomena and subject to the efficacy of sense perception.

In the view of the people of Bahá heaven and hell exist as an extension and result of our deeds. In other words, if the act is good it becomes in itself its own heaven and if not, it becomes its hell. However, since we believe in the everlasting life of the spirit, we say that this heaven or hell continues on past this physical realm of existence. In the other world, freed from physical limitations that prevent us from recognizing the heaven of good deeds and the hell of the bad ones we gain a new perception which gives us the ability to recognize and understand the impact of the nature of our deeds which we were incapable of determining while still in this physical world.

Which act, then, is its own heaven? The act that is devoid of attachment to any school of thought or social platform. It is the act that follows the wondrous and novel Bahá'í principles, enshrined in the *Aqdas*. Acts that are performed "for the love of My beauty."[3] Such an act is the very reality of heaven. Except that in this world it is not recognized as "the reality of heaven", but in the world of spirit it becomes clear that such an act has been, is and will be the very essence of heaven.

Returning to the philosophical interpretation of these concepts, we note that heaven and hell are basically associated with the concept of love rather than of intellect. Such an interpretation is derived from the principles of the Bahá'í Faith, which exalts love beyond all other phenomena. The Bahá'í Faith is a religion of love. As the intellect, though occupying such sublime rank, reaches its summit

---

[3] *Kitáb-i-Aqdas,* vers 4, p. 29.

of exaltation and abandons its conflicts with love, it can find a way to that ultimate threshold.

We should not be misguided into thinking that since we consider the nature of our deeds to be in and of themselves representative of the state of heaven or hell we can conclude, therefore, that there is no heaven or hell after the death of the body. 'Abdu'l-Bahá' has clearly rejected this view and has explained that if that had been the case he would not have been willing to endure so much hardship and pain in the path of service.[4]

---

[4] Tablet of 'Abdu'l-Bahá reproduced in Fázil Mázandaráni, *Amr va Khalq* (*Faith and Humanity;* untranslated) vol. 1.

10. Shahádat (Martyrdom) in the Bahá'í Faith

The word Shahádat in the Persian language means "to behold, to attain, to emerge or appear" (it also means martyrdom). The world that is invisible to our eyes is called the unseen kingdom and the world that appears before our eyes is called the world of *Shahádat* or the kingdom of the seen. Therefore *Sháhid* or *Shahíd* (which are alternate nouns or subject forms of the word *Shahádat*) refers to one who beholds with his eyes and recounts what he has seen. In other words,he has gained a knowledge that he shares with those who have not seen what he has. Because of his words, a matter unknown becomes known and a claim yet unfulfilled finds proof, so long as he remains Faithful to the truth of his assertion. Such a person is also known as a witness.

In the field of religion, *Shahádat* refers to a believer who bears witness and openly testifies to the truth of his religion as well as the inaugurator of that Faith. For example, in Islam such a believer would confess to the unity of God and the prophetic mission of Muhammad; a Bahá'í would bear witness to the unity of God and the manifestation of the Speaker on the Sinai.

The witness should also commit himself to the fulfillment of the duties contained in such a confession both in his physical and spiritual life. In other words, not only words should attest to the truthfulness of his confession but that his conduct, deeds and actions should support and corroborate his verbal commitment to his Faith. He should live his life such that each moment and each step of the way should demonstrate his Faithfulness to his beliefs and his devotion as a true witness to the truth of the Author of the Faith in Whom he has come to believe.

Given these conditions, his commitment or his act of bearing witness, will find constancy, will remain strong and will endure. And thus the word *shahíd* (martyr) which carries with it the qualities of constancy and endurance replaces the word *Sháhid* (he who beholds or bears witness) which is subject to the circumstances of time and place.

Thus it may be said that *Shahíd* is someone who throughout the passing years of his life remains Faithful and constant in his devotion to the truth and continues to bear witness to the verity of the Manifestation of the Cause he has espoused by his words, deeds and actions. His *Shahádat* thus opens the door of his heart and establishes a direct link with his life and at times the two become indistinguishable and therefore *Shahádat* becomes life and life, *Shahádat*. And these two phenomena, or should we say, this single phenomenon progresses gradually from the moment of one's confession of belief until the last moment of life without a moment's interruption.

From this discussion it is clear that *Shahíd* is not a specific and unique term that refers to those who sacrifice their lives in the path of their Faith; there are those who live in obscurity and tranquility and go through life without experiencing any conflicts or hostility and yet remain righteous and devoted throughout their lives. They eschew idle talk, misconduct and impure thoughts; invite everyone to the path of righteousness; arise to perform what is within their power in the path of service to the Cause; never tire in their endeavor; never abandon their enterprise; accept any loss peacefully and in utter contentment; entertain no fear of death, and yet, even though the swords of the villainous tyrants are not ordained to rain upon them and shed their blood, they pass their lives peacefully as nature had intended, and ultimately having dedicated their lives to the triumph of the Faith and service to the cause of humanity, close their eyes to this physical world.

These, too, pride themselves in having attained to the station of the *Shahíd* (Martyr) since during their lifetimes, they bore witness with their every act and word to the verity of their beliefs and bore proof to the unequivocal truth of God's Manifestation. Such a virtuous life has its source in unalloyed integrity and as it aspires to its level of perfection, it receives from the Most Great Pen the "reward of a hundred martyrs".[1]

The Blessed Beauty has bestowed this honor upon many believers who did not actually lose their lives in the path of service. Their names must be sought in history books.[2] And thus, in general, a life

---

[1] Reference to a passage in the Tablet of Ahmad, *Bahá'í Prayers.*

[2] As an example, hand of the Cause of God Ibn-i-Asdaq, asked Bahá'u'lláh to destine for him the honor of martyrdom. In a tablet Bahá'u'lláh has revealed the following: "God willing, with the utmost sanctity and purity, the Day of God, is to be witnessed and the exalted rank of martyrdom may be attained. Today, service to the Cause is considered a supreme achievement. Faithful friends, exercising absolute wisdom, must engage themselves in teaching the Cause of God, such that the fragrances of the divine raiment may be diffused in all directions. Martyrdom has not been limited to the act of giving up of life and physical sacrifice of self as it is possible that a believer possessing the bounty of physical life attain to such a rank in the sight of the Possessor of Names (in the path of service). Well is it with you who have expended your wealth, your possessions and whatever that is in your power in My path." 'Abdu'l-Bahá, in a tablet addresses Ibn-i-Asdaq reveals the following: "O' thou Exalted and Peerless Martyr: In this new era and wondrous century you have, praised be the Lord, arisen (in service) to whatever that is seemly and worthwhile..." Hand of the Cause Ibn-i-Asdaq ascended to the Abhá Kingdom in Tehran in 1924: Among those who have passed away of natural causes and yet have been honored as a "Martyr" is the renowned teacher of the Cause Miss Ransom-Kehler who, in October 23rd of 1933 in the 55th year of her life ascended to the Abhá kingdom in Isfahan and posthumously received the

spent in rendering certain services and acquiring spiritual virtues was considered by Him as equivalent to martyrdom, and those who attained such a station were regarded as martyrs. One such example is the services rendered by those who distinguish themselves by abandoning house and home and loved ones to pioneer in the path of God and pass away while at their posts.

> Verily those who journey as pioneers in the path of God and ascend to the Abhá Kingdom while at their posts, their names will be recorded by the Supreme Pen as martyrs in the path of God, the Mighty, the Everlasting.[3]

And yet what is more commonly intended by the word *Shahíd* is one who stands firm by the beliefs of his beloved Faith and continues, in the face of death to put forth proofs of its truth, remains undaunted at the fearful face of death, remains unyielding to the raised sword of the enemy, raises his head high and stands firm and unwavering, as the sword descends and strikes his neck severing his head from his body and turning the black earth crimson. This is the supreme station.

Those who have Faith thirst to be so tested, so that they may burn away this darksome and pitiful physical temple to which the precious gift of life has been bestowed and return to the exalted world of the spiritual reality and occupy the rank that only the acquired pristine qualities and unalloyed virtues can award. It is with this desire that their purity of motive is demonstrated through their martyrdom. Such a station has been considered by the Supreme Pen as the most exalted of all created virtues:

---

honor of becoming a Hand of the Cause of God as well as the rank of the first Western martyr.
[3] It is the text of a verse of the Ancient Beauty which has been quoted in the message of the Universal House of Justice, dated Aug. 22, 1972 addressed to the NSA of Iran. See *Letters of the Universal House of Justice*, vol., p. 294.

10. Shahádat (Martyrdom) in the Bahá'í Faith

O' Son of Man

By My Beauty! To tinge thy hair with thy blood is greater in my sight than the creation of the universe and the light of both worlds. Strive then to attain this O' servant![4]

Martyrdom, in various religious traditions and at different historical times has manifested itself in multiple forms. At times in combat and assuming a defensive posture, there have been warriors who, in the path of God and in defense of the truth have raised their swords and shields and have been beheaded and thus lost their lives sacrificially. The martyrs of Karbala in Islamic history, the martyrs of Mazindarán and Nayríz and Zanján in the Bábí period are examples of such pure hearted lovers of God.

At other times a lover, without taking up a weapon, is killed; without the slightest threat of violence is brought down to dust; without the least intention to fight, is beheaded; without raising a hand is decapitated; without any sign of aggression is slain. In such a case, on the one hand, tyranny reaches its summit; the heart of the enemy turns into rock; innocents lose their lives; honor loses its meaning, the human creature degenerates into utter depravity of a desert vulture; he becomes *Hájib'ud'Dulih* (killer of Amir Kabir, Naseridin Shah's prime minister and a great statesman whose arteries were cut open, while in the bathhouse, by the Shah's order and bled to death), Son of the Wolf and *Zillu'l-Sultan* (Governor of Isfahán and responsible for the death of unnumbered Bahá'ís-Translator).[5]

On the other hand, the supreme power of Faith is demonstrated, as nothing can tarnish or defile the staunch love of the unwavering lover. Whenever the Faithful believer arises to fight, his act of combat may be motivated by the hope of tasting ultimate victory.

---

[4] *Hidden Words of Bahá'u'lláh,* Arabic, verse 47.
[5] References to the lives of Hajib, Son of the Wolf and Zillus-Sultán are found in the Persian edition of the book *The Choice Wine* (untranslated).

111

It is easy to wonder if he risks his life in order to gain material recompense and that he rushes into the killing field to find worldly glory? In such a case would he remain steadfast even in the face of certain defeat; would he then reject the love of the Beloved and abandon his spiritual quest in order to save his life? Thus risking life in such a circumstance and by such a one is not evidence of selfless sacrifice. If such a warrior were to resort to deceit, intrigue, conspiracy and dissimulation, we could surmise him to be nothing more than an inhuman, ill intentioned and crafty individual since he does not concern himself with dishonesty, duplicity and trickery. He becomes a deceitful hypocrite since not only does he abandon his own Faith but in order to reach his goal he goes so far as to belittle, disgrace and dishonor its principles and in so doing brings himself down to utter misery and ignominy. In case of his death, no honor or glory will accompany such an act of seeming sacrifice.

And yet what can we say about an individual who without weapon, without any intention to either attack or defend stands before the bloodthirsty enemy, fearlessly holds his head high and firmly plants his feet and undaunted bares his neck to the sword and smilingly yields himself to death as he refuses to violate the covenant of love to which he has committed himself; he falls in the dust in his own blood and yet does not break the cord of affection and spiritual attachment. Then who can presume to call such a martyr a hypocrite or hesitate in accepting the truth of a Faith for the love of which he has accepted the supreme sacrifice? Read the history of the martyrs of Yazd so that you may witness the power of the Faith of Bahá'u'lláh and the sacrificial acts of those exemplars of honor and holiness.[6]

At times, martyrdom is due to accident or is the result of intense attraction. The intensity of love is so great as to render the lover

---

[6] *History of the Martyrs of Yazd* is the name of a book by Muhammad Táhir Málmírí which covers the lives, services and martyrdoms of the believers of Yazd and its environs. The work has been published in Persian.

senseless, taking away from him his will power and making him unafraid of dangers he will face in arising to serve. In his love for the truth, he closes his eyes to the wisdom of things and moves forward unafraid. His heart is filled with the love of the Beloved, and heedless of the risks awaiting him, unwittingly and unintentionally he falls to his death. The ecstasy of love is so all-consuming that his control over life and limb is lost. The hand of destiny removes the veil of the material existence from the countenance of his spirit so that he may discover his Beloved with the eye of his soul. His death is the sign of his detachment and intense love. This detachment flows from the power of the divine Word and this attraction is the result of the intensity of true love. Such an individual, with his death, bears witness to the creativeness of the word of God and proves the claim of the truth of his love. The Purest Branch, who issued from the Divine Lote Tree, may be considered the supreme example of this category of the martyrs of the Faith:

> The mention of God and His praise and the praise of the denizens of the Kingdom of Eternity and the Kingdom of Names be upon thee. Happy art thou for having remained Faithful to the covenant of God and His commandments and sacrificed thy self before the face of thy Lord, the loving and powerful.[7]

The truth is that the martyrs yearn for martyrdom; they can discern eternal life awaiting them on the other side of physical death. They see the physical body as an obstacle to their nearness to God; they consider such state of nearness as the only true life and regard life in this world as a prison of their souls. However, they do not consider taking their own lives or deliberately placing themselves in the path of death as befitting since they have been admonished by the Beloved of hearts and souls in these terms:

> Lovers of God should not become agitated and frightened, but should consider martyrdom in the path of the Friend as grace

---

[7] Reference to a portion of the Tablet of Visitation for the Purest Branch, revealed by Bahá'u'lláh.

abounding. That is only if it so happens and not that the friends should place themselves in the path of death.[8]

Plato's interpretation of the subject is that He who, willfully, releases himself from this earthly life is like a soldier who prior to receiving his orders from his superior, leaves his post, or a servant who against his master's direction abandons the place of his service, even though, both the soldier and the servant may do this in the hope of attaining the presence of their master. The body, therefore, must be kept safe although it is a barrier for the spirit. This earthly life should not be considered ignoble though it impedes attaining the threshold of the Beloved.

The power of the physical body must be used to tread the path of love; the life in this world must provide the capital for the future transaction of spiritual gain. Such martyrs do not give up life willfully; they make sure that the material body receives the best care and is kept from harm as far as possible; they confront hardship and adversity, rise and strive to the best of their abilities, engage themselves in making a living and do not sit idly by but continue to press forward. Yet they do not fear the raised sword of the enemy if their every effort to avoid such a destiny has proven futile. They consider such a death as an invitation for attaining the presence of the Beloved. Before the bloodthirsty murderer they do not become submissive, dispirited and groveling; they look beyond death and happily and hopefully place their necks before the sword.

> I have sent death as a messenger of joy to thee; wherefore dost thou grieve ?[9]

Those who meet death joyfully witness to the eternal nature of the human spirit. They stand as proof of the existence of life in the kingdom of God; with their death they say to others that beyond the

---

[8] From the tablet of "Pisar-i-'Amm" (Cousin), *Iqtidárát* (compilation; untranslated), p, 179.
[9] Reference to the *Hidden Words of Bahá'u'lláh,* Arabic, verse 32.

grave they have seen the signs of eternal life; by their actions they prove that the Faith of God penetrates the hearts and souls of the Faithful. The Word of God is creative and its truth is in its creativity. It is because of this that the sanctified blood that is shed in the path of God has such an enormous influence in the world of the spirit; it makes the tree of Faith stronger, fruitful and a provider of shade; it raises the message of the Beloved to the summit of heavens. It is because of this creativity of the Word of God that the martyrdom of the Husayn-ibn-'Alí becomes the preserver of the Faith of Islam; martyrdom of the Primal Point is, in itself, the proclamation of the Faith of Bahá'u'lláh; the martyrdom of Badí' exalts him to the level of a "new creation"; the tale of the martyrdom of the King of the Martyrs makes of him the "Ornament of the Book of Fidelity" and it is because of this that the Guardian of the Ancient Beauty addressing the people of the world says:

> It is the shedding of the sanctified blood of the Iranian martyrs, that in this illumined century and this most glorious age will transform this earth into the eternal paradise and shall hoist the tabernacle of the unity of human race, as revealed in the Tablets, to the summit of farthest horizons and manifest the principle of unity and establish world peace, make this nether world the mirror image of Abhá paradise and prove to the world the truth of: "that day this earth will become a different earth".[10]

---

[10] From the *Persian Letters of the Guardian*, Ridván 1989, vol. 2, p. 252.

11. Free Will

The concept of "Free Will" is among the principle beliefs of the People of Bahá. Not only do we consider man free to choose, but from amongst all creatures in the world of existence, we regard man unique in the exercise of such a power. By free will it is meant that man is free to want and then take the necessary action in order to realize or satisfy that desire; at the same time he is also capable of deciding to reject a certain desire and therefore choose not to take any action in its fulfillment.

Other creatures, unlike man, are incapable of exercising the power of free will since the inanimate, the vegetable and the animal grades of existence are governed by nature; as their physical make up is material and unchanging, they act in accordance with the requirements of the component elements of that make- up. Even the vegetable and animal life, as per Abdu'l-Bahá's teaching, is devoid of what may be considered a spiritual dimension or an essence that could be regarded as anything other than the manifestation of its physical existence.[1]

The Bahá'í Writings do contain references to vegetable, mineral and animal spirits. However, when the word "spirit" is used no "non-physical spiritual" state is intended. In His discussion of this subject matter 'Abdu'l-Bahá offers proof of the concept of spirit

---

[1] Reference to *Some Answered Questions,* "Immortality of the Spirit," pp. 223-227.

only when the human spirit is considered. The "spirit", as it relates to the vegetable and animal life forms, finds its meaning only in their physical expression. 'Abdu'l-Bahá explains that as the component elements of this material make-up disintegrate, its spirit too declines and fades. Thus, all grades of existence below the human level, are strictly material and attached to the world of nature and subject to the material requirements and essential dictates of the world of nature.

Spiritualists believe that, in accordance with God's will, the inanimate, the vegetable, and the animal follow a pre-ordained path; they are deprived of the capability to exercise the power of choice and therefore can never alter the path that has been selected for them. There is only one way for them to follow, and they cannot choose otherwise; because of this lack of choice, the ethical or moral concepts of good and bad cannot be applicable to them. We can never say that what an animal did was bad or good because it did what it had to do; doing otherwise was not a choice it could make. So any discussion regarding the concept of "Free Will" as applicable to all creatures that fall below the human level of existence becomes futile and absurd.

In levels higher than that of man (angels and such) good and bad are also inapplicable; the power of God always flows in the direction of good, and thus the concept of "bad" loses its meaning. Therefore in the higher kingdom or the manifold worlds of God, the two qualities of good and bad become inapplicable. Since reference was made to angels, it should be made clear that we do not recognize angels as human-like creatures who are composed of material elements and appear with wings and feathers and take on a lighter appearance and yet possess a natural and material body. Our interpretation of angels is spiritual. Sometimes we ascribe this angelic condition to those we know to be pure of heart and deed who live among us, and at times to the spirits of such heavenly ones who have already ascended, and yet at other times to the invisible divine power through which God's will is done on earth. In no wise, however, do we believe angels to be corporeal or human-like.[2]

Man is placed between two poles: one is the pole of pure goodness where evil has no meaning, where relative perfection is evinced when no human deficiency or shortcoming can be discerned; the second pole shows that man is capable of doing evil, and yet his deeds may not necessarily be evil as he does what he is obligated to do and cannot do otherwise. Man is, then, placed between these two poles where good and bad find meaning; where personal will comes into play, and the power to choose a certain action emerges. We not only consider man to be endowed with the power of choice but to be, in fact. The only created being that is so empowered. Of course, Authors of the eternal Faiths of God who are perfect human beings have such a power in its perfect form. 'Abdu'l-Bahá tells us that since these Manifestations of God possess all human perfections, whatever human qualities and virtues that appear in man exist in the Manifestations in their perfect form.[3] Thus, the power of free will that exists in the manifestations of Divine Will appears in them in its perfect and exalted form, and, as such, it takes on a different character from the imperfect condition that exists in man. It is due to man's imperfect and limited nature that human free-will is the initiator of the path towards good or evil.

However, when we consider the matter as it relates to God, we discover that He cannot be regarded as being conditioned by free will or its lack; such a condition can only find meaning within the sphere of human life. In the Divine, qualities are the same as His essential reality rather than being independent attributes. However, in the world of existence where qualities are apart from realities the

---

[2] References to original texts regarding the concept of "Angels" see the book *Rahíq-i-Makhtúm* (*The Choice Wine;* untranslated) and Má'dih-i-Ásmání (*Heavenly Sustenance;* untranslated).

[3] *Some Answered Questions.*

qualities can emerge as independent attributes in various forms such as free will.

Given this definition of free will we find man unique in possessing such power and regard no other creature to be so endowed. As man is the manifestation of the perfections of God, he is also the manifestation of the attribute of free will. Of course, when we say that a "human being" has free will we don't mean that such a power is all embracing; his being is not entirely "human". If a human being consisted of pure spirit, devoid of a physical entity, that would have allowed such spiritual power to have appeared in humankind in perfect form. However, a human being is a combination of spirit (soul) and matter (physical body composed of matter) and therefore subject to the laws that govern the world of matter and subordinate to the requirements of nature.

The human body is a combination of blood, flesh, skin and bone. How can such a combination be free from the dictates of natural laws that govern them? Man is also a vegetable. He has within him the attributes of a vegetable life such as respiration, growth and procreation. These are attributes that are essential to his life and his survival, and he has no choice but to comply with their requirement. In addition, man is also an animal. He possesses sense perception, enjoys mobility and freedom within limitations that are applicable to the animal. In so far as the power of sense perception is concerned, man is an animal and is thus powerless to resist nature's laws. His eyes will see, his ears will hear, and he is unable to control them in so far as animal life dictates their use.

A human being is not only human but is subject to the dictates of nature. Obviously, if we define man in these terms we could never attach to him the power of free will as he would be completely ruled by the laws of nature. This definition of a human being is the belief of those who only consider man in such a light.

We, however, as human beings, recognize and understand the requirements and limitations of our mineral, vegetable and animal dimensions. The understanding and awareness that we develop of these conditions is absent in the mineral, vegetable or animal, and it is because of this sense of recognition that we are capable of restricting the dictates of our animal existence and exercising our free will. This condition, in effect, enables us to control the animalistic whims and desires that rule the world of nature. We realize this ability as we recognize in ourselves a power of consciousness or awareness that we do not find in other creatures. This condition of consciousness accompanies our every state or action and gives it a dual effect. A vegetable respires, but man respires and is aware that he is breathing. An animal sees, or becomes angry or fearful, but a human being sees, becomes angry and fearful and also has a dominating awareness that he sees, is angry and fearful. In effect, every condition in man has a twofold expression in which the first corroborates the second. Such a condition is unique to man and is a measure of his distinction over the animal. This awareness gives man the power of free will; consciousness activates the free will. Consciousness is not free will itself but is the condition that triggers the operation of free will.

Free will itself is a condition which we sense without needing to prove its existence. Those who deny the existence of free will must prove their view point since they are the ones who express a condition which is contrary to human senses.

Now, how does man sense this power of free will in himself? In two stages: first by the doubt or hesitation he entertains before initiating an action. Should I do this or not? Should I say this or not? Should I go or stay? All such conditions demonstrate man's free will to choose one of the two options. Secondly, the regret or contentment he feels following completion of a certain action, which highlight his state of remorse or satisfaction at the result of that action. This two-stage process denotes that he has been free to choose and, depending on the result obtained, is either displeased or happy. The moment we feel remorse at an action we become aware that we could have done otherwise; this remorse clearly demonstrates the power of free will.

If, however, we commit a certain act through coercion or while under the influence of drugs, we will experience no feelings of remorse even if we commit murder. In this condition the only feeling of regret is: why did I place myself in a condition that caused my free will to be compromised which, in turn, lead to the act? The only misgiving in such a situation is channeled to that part of the action for which we exercised free will. This condition of free will is so strong in us that we protest if we are deprived of its exercise. If someone tries to make decisions for us in disregard of our choice, we object strenuously and exclaim: "I am a human being and capable of making that decision myself." In other words, we recognize our free will as an indication of our humanness, and the proof of its existence is doubt before action and remorse at its result. Not only do these two conditions provide clear evidence of the existence of free will in man but also signify its limits within the sphere of moral issues. Free will pertains to conditions we can classify as "right" or "wrong" or acts that call for "reward" or "punishment" regardless of whether they are dictated by one's conscience, social law or religious principle. Thus, it is within the purview of such issues that doubt and regret find meaning. Free will signifies the existence of responsibility. Where moral responsibility has no role to play, free will has no application. We call to mind 'Abdu'l-Bahá's striking principle: "The limits of free will are the limits of moral responsibility".[4]

One may feel this moral responsibility towards one's self, one's family, one's country, one's kind, or towards the human race or towards God. In whatever way it may emerge, responsibility necessitates free will. Since according to Bahá'í belief, man is

---

[4] Reference the *Compilation of Tablets of 'Abdu'l-Bahá.*

endowed with a human spirit he is capable of exercising certain measure of freedom from the dictates of nature and material constraints. Free will stems from such a matrix and is limited to it. Therefore, those who do not believe in the existence of a human spirit in man can easily disregard the existence of free will.

Of course there are those, i.e. existentialists, who disbelieve in the human spirit but do believe in free will. Such conceptual contradiction is untenable according to both principle and logic; perhaps that is why the believers in such a theory have never been able to leave a lasting impression of their belief system.

We believe man is endowed with the human spirit, a condition that is unique in the world of creation and is different from the mineral, vegetable and animal spirits. The human spirit is not material and not physical and as such will endure after the destruction of the human body. Its nature is not known because our impression of it originates from our natural sense perception, and any such perception will obviously take on a natural or material appearance. Thus we are unable to perceive it as it really is. No one can say I have either felt or had a vision of my spirit. One can perceive its existence but not its essence. 'Abdu'l-Bahá has told us that both God and spirit can be perceived, and those who are able to apprehend the reality of the spirit have no need for its proof.[5]

The evidences that demonstrate the existence of the spirit are manifold. One is the awareness that accompanies our every physical condition (consciousness). While we can say that such physical conditions as fear, anger, vision or hearing are in themselves products of bodily functions such as the operation of the nervous system, various glands or other physical activities, yet the condition of "awareness" that accompanies these functions has no physical

---

[5] *Some Answered Questions,* "Free Will," p. 248.

source or center. Therefore, such a phenomenon is not a physical condition.

Another evidence of soul's existence is free will, which is possessed by man and yet has no physical originator or prime mover in his physical body. Love is also a distinct indication. This love is free from lust, entirely unconditional, and completely selfless-- not a possessive type of love that is governed by self interest and aims at material gain. 'Abdu'l-Bahá has been very emphatic that the power of discovery is additional evidence of the main distinction of man over animal.[6] This power which enables man to discover an unknown from known parameters does not have a physical or natural source and is unique to man. These and other non-tangible forces are the evidences that differentiate man from the animal.

When we say that we believe in the human soul as a non-physical entity, we mean that we believe the soul to be the source or the motive force for the appearance of these unique powers; because of this we do not consider man as strictly animal or a transformed version of other animals. This, of course, introduces the whole subject of evolution which expresses belief in the transformation of animals from one species to another, concluding in the appearance of the human form. We do not deny the fact that man has been subject to the process of evolution. It is clear that his appearance has not always been the same as it is today which is in accordance with the evolutionary theory. However, since a human being is "human" due to the existence of his soul, we believe that while his body may have gone through considerable changes over time, he cannot be considered the evolved version of any other animal; regardless of the transformation of his physical features, it is the possession of the human soul that identifies him as a human and not the form or appearance of his physical body.

---

[6] *Some Answered Questions,* "Difference between Man and Animal."

To understand this, consider the example of the reflection of the sun's light in a mirror. In order to produce a clear and shiny reflection of the light, it is essential that the mirror be made of a specific combination of elements. It should be made of a special glass with a specially selected substance spread over its surface making it capable of reflecting the light of the sun. The mirror must first become the recipient of the beams of sunlight before it can reflect its rays. It should be clear that the phenomenon of the reflection of light is principally due to the shining of the sun's beams and not to the mirror, which without such light is nothing but glass. Man's body has the same relationship with his soul. The body must reach a prescribed level of physical maturity before it can reflect the light of the spirit, which is a divine reality and an independent creation. Thus, the evolution of man's physical body is a process that according to Bahá'í belief simply helps it to reach a level of growth and maturity enabling it to reflect the light of that external source we call "spirit" or "rational soul". Therefore, man is man because of the existence of his soul and cannot be the evolved version of any animal. What may one day be ultimately proven is that the body of man, as it is today, is the product of the process of gradual evolution; however, his soul remains independent to such a natural process and is the handiwork of the Divine; this soul becomes attached to the human body and makes of him a human being.

Thus, we put aside the idea that man has only an animal side and consider him God's handiwork, a super natural creation and an exalted being in this lower level of existence. That is what we believe regarding man's station; he is the possessor of free will with all its attendant responsibilities. Possessing free will man can no longer claim that he is helplessly subject to the changes and chances of the world, or claim that he is devoid of any real power to change himself or what is around him, or that he is totally powerless before the dominating force of nature. We see him as one who can arise, stand on his own feet and determine his own destiny.

It is here that morality comes to the fore and exerts itself in our lives. Any notion of morality had been dismissed due to man's view of his sole animal existence. It now emerges and enables him to become the manifestation of God's virtues and perfections and become free to keep or abandon such perfections; in so doing, through the operation of his conscience, he feels the weight of responsibility.

Once such a belief is established, man no longer considers himself as entirely mortal with the death of his body since mortality is specific to physical and material things. Since man's soul is not material and physical, it will continue to endure after the destruction of the body.

12. Harmony of Science and Religion

Another subject that has to be discussed as it concerns religion is the essential harmony between religion and science. There has been a great misunderstanding regarding this matter; the issue has been wrongly grasped, completely misconstrued, incorrectly interpreted and, therefore, has lead to irrelevant conclusions. The misunderstandings include: that religion is identical to intellect or reason; that science and intellect are capable of eliminating the need for religion; that religion is the same as science, and other such conclusions.

In the Middle Ages religion and science were in conflict with each other in such a way that Faith and intellect were in opposite camps; whatever Faith required was different from what intellect specified. The attempt was made to make the intellect subordinate to Faith, to be a servant of Faith. The intellect was expected to analyze, interpret and judge as Faith required. The decree of the intellect was measured against the requirement of Faith. And thus if a conflict appeared, intellect was abandoned and the scholar or the scientist was denounced, anathematized, killed or burned alive for holding views contrary to the dictates of Faith. Any thought or word which was not in line with the basic precepts of religion and Faith was sufficient cause for excommunication of the accused. All aspects of life were determined in accordance with the dictates of religion; even in astronomy, natural sciences, principles of exploitation of mines and sciences related to plant and animal life, the decree of religion was final and intellect made its determination subject to the findings of religion. This was also true in every day trade and the commercial activities of people. In short religion specified, in detail, the rules and regulation governing each and every facet of everyday life. There was even an applicable rule for visiting the toilet and the cleaning of oneself which included an incantation to be recited. The rule equally applied to other occasions. For example, upon detecting the fragrance of a rose, one had to recite a particular incantation. It is said that once a man confused the two incantations and while in the toilet, recited the verse: "O' God waft upon us the heavenly fragrances of paradise!"

The intention here is to show that in the Middle Ages, all acts and thoughts, manners, traditions and conditions carried with it a religious connotation and thus nothing was left to the dictate of the intellect. This condition was even more intense in Christian Europe. In Christianity, many rules and principles of conduct are not clearly defined in the Bible; therefore, the established principles of the Church were accepted as a requirement of obedience and Faithfulness without any attempt at a logical evaluation or explanation. In other words, being a Christian required a complete negation of logical interpretation or intellectual expression. Because of this ban on scientific thought in the Middle Ages, secularism had its beginnings in Christian Europe.

The fiercest reaction to religion took place in Europe during the Renaissance.[1] This was perhaps due to the excessively restrictive measures that had been placed in the path of intellectual expression

---

[1] The word "Renaissance" which in Persian has been rendered as "Tajdíd-i-Hayát" or "Rebirth" is a label that defines the revolutionary transformation in various facets of life in the 14th through 16th centuries in Europe. This rebirth was initiated in Italy in the 14th century and reached its zenith in the 15th and 16th centuries across Europe. It revolutionized the worlds of industry, art, sciences, literature and education across the entire continent.

at the time. You may consider Martin Luther, who established the Protestant Faith and openly arose against the dictatorial power of the Catholic Church, as the promulgator of liberal and progressive thought and possibly the inaugurator of religious freedom in Europe.[2]

And yet when one takes a good look at his teachings, one realizes the irony of the situation. His rebellion, in fact, was based on his disagreement with the church for incorporating into church teachings, within the thousand years of the Middle Ages, a whole host of intellectual concepts which in his view discredited the Bible. He demanded their removal so that only the original teachings of the New Testament would be binding. All prevalent concepts that stemmed from the philosophy of Greek masters or even the traditional church interpretations, which had crept into routine religious practices of the time, had to be abandoned; only the basic teachings of the Bible were to be preached, listened to and obeyed.

Luther's disdain for the utilization of the intellect for the issuance of a sacred writ may be readily discerned from a metaphor he offers to express his view. He says that "the mind is like a prostitute" since it makes little difference to the mind in what manner or for what purpose it is used. The mind will serve the thief to improve his craft; it assists a doctor to improve his medical practice, helps the righteous in his acts of charity and aids the thief to better his criminal designs. Therefore the mind can serve any objective without regard to its ultimate result and that is why it is likened to a prostitute. It is thus to be set aside and its judgment disregarded. The basic dictates of religion and Faith should be considered as the true and ultimate guide. This, then, was the prison within which the mind became captive.

---

[2] Martin Luther was the German religious reformer who founded the protestant Faith and rose against the religious rule of the Catholic Church. Luther was born in 1483 and died in 1546.

I earlier mentioned the fact that in Islam the principles of religion must be accepted through the faculty of the mind; otherwise ones confession of belief is not acceptable; yet the mind has to arrive at the same conclusion reached by Faith, otherwise the believer would have to forfeit his life. Suppose ones intellectual examination led him to deny the existence of God. Such a man would have to be killed or made to recant as his conclusion would not be in line with the dictates of religion. If a devotee decided that his logic could not accept the idea that Muhammad sealed the line of prophethood, he would be labeled an apostate and would have to die. Thus the mind is to be utilized to determine and judge, and yet such a judgment has to be in compliance with the dictates of religion. It is clear that in all facets of life the mind has been made captive to the wishes of religion, life's unique and singular sustaining pillar.

With the emergence of new sciences the reverse of this attitude began to prevail. The mind excommunicated religion. The mind asserted that religion had to move to one side so that mind could become the governing judge on all issues. In other words, with the power of the mind and its fruit (the sciences) there is no further need for religion. That is the call of Western civilization. The mind comes from man; science comes from the mind; industry comes from science; through this process man is capable of resolving any and all problems. Through his scientific discoveries he conquers the world of nature and dominates its laws.

In the area of the moral and spiritual relationship between human beings, the judgment of the mind is adequate. Religion appears superfluous as science can easily play the role of religion as science has dominated all other aspects of life.

Science and religion are in conflict. They can neither be conciliated nor done away with. One of the two has to remain while the other one has to be destroyed. When this one arrives, there is no room for that one; there is only room for religion or for the mind. Thus when the Bahá'í Faith asserts the need for both religion and science to come into agreement with each other, it intends to remove this conflict and harmonize their purposes. The teachings of the Faith explain that it is not necessary for one to take the place of the other, that there is enough room for both, and each has to occupy its own place. Religion, with its unique approach, has its own place and its own jurisdiction, and science, with its own unique approach, has its appointed place and its area of application. If a religion asserts that we should obey its dictates alone and dispense with science and whatever comes from the intellect, then that religion is untrue. If the mind claims to have the final say on all issues, then that claim is also false.

These two forces are compatible and in agreement. Note that I emphasize these adjectives as both have been used in various tablets. When we say that religion and science should be in agreement, we don't mean that they are the same or that one is the same as the other. Two things can be of different nature and yet be compatible with each other. They are different from each other but are not in conflict with each other. Not only are they not in conflict, they are, in fact, in agreement. Consider this podium and this microphone. These two are totally different from each other, but they are not in conflict with each other. In fact they are in total agreement as one is the support of the other. Thus, the agreement between two things does not necessitate that they should be the same. When we say science and religion are in agreement, we mean they are not in conflict; we do not mean they are the same or that we can expect from one the same thing that we expect from the other. The work of religion is not the work of science; the purpose of religion is not the same of that of science; the approach of religion is not the approach of science; we should understand the distinction and not make the mistake others have. The current belief of the "champions of the pulpit" (denotes clergy-Translator) are misguided if they see all the scientific and industrial inventions and discoveries as byproducts of religion.

Surely you must have attended a religious gathering and have witnessed what the man who climbs the pulpit preaches. There is no longer any reference to traditions, no mention of holy verses, no talk of the eternal world, and no sign of anything spiritual. He talks about space crafts, intercontinental missiles, atomic bombs and Darwin's evolutionary theory without having an iota of knowledge about any of them.[3]

Science does not lend itself to humor; it has specific and exact principles, complex formulas which must be studied by experts and by those who have spent their entire lives studying them. An expert in the construction of spacecraft does not take it upon himself to render judgment on the concept of evolution. But these champions of the pulpit boldly speak on all such subjects and spare no effort to somehow stitch these developments to the principles of religion intimating that all such matters have existed in religion and now science is only confirming what religion foreshadowed a long time ago. We must not make this mistake.

We should not enter into a discussion on atomic physics based on our knowledge of the Aqdas or vice versa. Our understanding of the science of chemistry should not be expressed with the language of the Iqán. This is neither a service to science nor to religion. Although God's Manifestation may have made mention of a scientific point, it was not His intention to make of any scientific phenomenon a religious concept. In that circumstance, He is like any other individual who simply wishes to express a certain view point about a scientific point using the language of science which is no different than explaining an historical event from a certain view point. So

---

[3] Dr. Dávúdí is referring to the Islamic religious meetings of his time when it had become fashionable for the preachers to list scientific discoveries or inventions and attribute their appearance to religious teachings (Translator).

132

let us not attempt to either find scientific explanations for religious beliefs or derive religious confirmation for scientific principles.

Now, why is this so?

Actually it is quite easy to understand. Scientific judgment is typically provisional as its findings are mostly relative, contingent and inconclusive. What today is called scientific truth could easily be regarded as false in fifty years. What is a fair man to do in fifty years if his critical comparison of today's scientific findings against religious truth is no longer relevant as newly found data alter science's road map and lead him in a whole different direction?

Scientific truth is not absolute as determinations are made on the basis of research conducted up to a certain time and therefore cannot be regarded as conclusive and final or viewed as entirely true. Sometime scientific truth shows us a small fragment of a "fact" while it is unmindful of the entire truth. Therefore he who wishes to corroborate a religious truth with the support of a scientific theory, that is obviously limited by the conditions of time and place, has not served the cause of religion and should not expect to find confirmation of religious teachings through scientific findings. If one does this, it would be as if he expected to receive the same result from this podium as he did from this microphone. These two are different from each other and yet are in harmony. If religion acts contrary to science and intellect, it has done badly and has taken the wrong path. Religion must be compatible with science and intellect while, at the same time, being different from it.

The contrary case is also true. If science finds itself in conflict with religion, it, too, has gone astray. So let science do its own work, express itself in its own terms, make its own discoveries, go its own way, advance at its own pace. If we do this, science will never be found to be in contention with true religion. Whatever is examined and researched through scientific methodology, will never be in

133

conflict or incompatible with the basic principles of religion. Some of the unfavorable or negative references made to certain scientific theories only concern the faulty conclusions that have been derived from these theories and have nothing to do with science itself. 'Abdu'l-Bahá's disagreement with Darwin's theory rests on the principle that the scientific conclusion that considers the entirety of human existence as a physical phenomenon, albeit, on a higher evolutionary scale, is not valid. It is due to His intention to reject this unscientific conclusion that He has expressed disagreement with the theory and not to the scientific theory itself.[4]

Such a conclusion brings the human creation down to the level of the animal and divests his nature of a spiritual and heavenly aspect; such a conclusion leads to a clear denial of an eternal spirit and subjugates him to the laws of nature, invalidating his supernatural and non-physical character; such a conclusion makes of him a captive to the laws of the jungle. Such conclusions, prescribing for man the struggle to survive, to fight, to compete and to conquer, are unscientific views which have been proffered in the name of science and are, in fact, unscientific conclusions.

Various camps hold various views on Darwin's theory as they themselves differ in their approach and wish to interpret science in such a way as to prove their point. From the handful of principles theorized by Darwin, Western scholars in the field of biology deny the transfer of acquired attributes as a hereditary condition. The biologists of the Soviet Union (this address was given when Soviet Union was a world power during the cold war years-Translator) accept the heredity principle but deny the struggle for survival. Why? Because each group believes in the theory that is most closely in line with its own ideological principles. Competing scientific

---

[4] To review 'Abdu'l-Bahá's works on this issue see *Some Answered Questions*, "Modification of Species," p. 177, and *Makatíb-i-'Abdu'l-Bahá* (*Tablet of 'Abdu'l-Bahá; untranslated*).

communities try to tailor science to suit their adopted political systems and express their views as scientific conclusions.

'Abdu'l-Bahá, when He chooses to point out such misperceptions, typically indicates that the scholars will in time discover their error. In other words, He wishes for them to continue their work until they, independently and through their own research, uncover the truth rather than having to be influenced by His judgment as a religious leader. They will uncover the truth in due course. 'Abdu'l-Bahá does not consider it permissible to use religious considerations to obstruct or impede the scientific search after truth. What He has brought awareness to are the faulty and unscientific conclusions that have been put forward.

So I have attempted to show that science does not present a way to the ultimate truth at any given time and if we try to harmonize religion and science at such a time we would, in fact, debase religion in our seeming attempt to serve its purpose. When we say religion must be compatible with logic and science what is it that we mean exactly. The mind that has expended all its energy and has discovered the ultimate truth will be compatible with the religion which through divine revelation has shown the way to that same reality. Science only finds the whole truth when it has completed its journey of research and discovery and not by offering a theory today which will have to be revised, adjusted, corrected, or negated in twenty years.

The intellect that is capable of understanding all truth will, of course, be compatible with religion. However, such a highly developed mind is only attainable once it has traversed and completed its evolutionary process and proved the results of its discovery beyond any doubt; such a mind does not just suddenly emerge without having scaled the evolutionary ladder.

If the entire truth comes to light, then no further conflict with religion will remain; at such a time we can say that science and religion are in fact compatible.

An example of this is the science of astronomy. At one time it was an accepted theorem that the sun revolved around the earth, and our senses testified to such a system. When we say a chair is brown, we make that decision based on our senses; the brown color can readily be seen leaving no doubt in any mind regarding the color of the chair. No one can argue with the decree of the senses. When the idea that the earth revolved around the sun was proposed, the people cried in horror as that idea was clearly against the judgment of the senses and the mind. Scientific truths continue to adjust, change and improve with scientific findings, and this process knows no end.

Thus, we must achieve the ultimate truth of a scientific theory or idea before its compatibility with religion can be evaluated. Since this is not possible, science should not play a decisive role in favor of or in opposition to religious concepts. We must be aware not to make the following mistakes:

1. The decree of reason should not be denied.

2. The validity of science should not be questioned.

3. Science should not be abandoned if its judgment is other than that of religious beliefs.

4. Intellectual judgment should not be evaluated based on religious pronouncements.

5. Science should be left free to discover the essential relationships between physical phenomena based on the decree of reason. Science should be free to discover the connection between pressure and weight, between pressure and volume, between heat and expansion, between heat and light; in the plant

and animal worlds science should investigate the relationship between respiration and combustion, between heat and the blood circulatory system, between nourishment and growth, between various aspects of the nervous system; in the human psyche science should investigate the relationship between fear and anger, between agitation and despair, between despair and debility. This is the work of science and scientists should be free to pursue it. However if science makes claims in other realms, it has exceeded its limits of authority and will not succeed.

Now let us investigate the purpose of religion. Religion is to satisfy the highest hopes and fulfill the foremost aspirations of the human family. It should create confidence, bestow upon man the precious gift of Faith and keep him contented and peaceful so that in the midst of turmoil, unrest and upheaval his trust and reliance should be focused on the bounty of the ultimate reality. In all fairness science is unable to achieve such a goal. For three or four hundred years it has tried and failed. It has only proven that as the role of science advanced, there has been a marked increase in humanity's turmoil, chaos and the number of suicides.

In this field, the work that a lowly priest can do by visiting the members of his flock and creating hope and assurance in their hearts or the words that a simple *Murshid* (Muslim spiritual leader) can say in a place of worship that will touch the hearts of his listeners, cannot be performed by the greatest and most exalted scientific scholars. The evidence for this claim is that science has never been able to create confidence in the hearts of man. It has succeeded to reason and this reason has brought with it chaos or suppression or it has led to disorder or autocracy. The mind has not yet found a third option. This is because science has wished to be the single and unique arbiter. Intellect has desired to be exclusive, assuming that whatever has proven to be beneficial in one place should be applicable everywhere. Intellect has not recognized its limitation.

12. Harmony of Science and Religion

In the name of science Intellect has proposed to forgo the concept of chastity to obviate ensuing problems that might emerge and remain unsolvable. In other words let us disregard the problem so that its solution should not prove to be beyond the limits of science's capacity. Hitler proposed to solve the Jewish problem by killing every Jew. This way there would remain no problem to solve.

The psychologists who have prescribed the removal of all limits on sexual practice have been oblivious of the fact that human beings are not animals and that the sexual urge in man has passed the limits of instinctive behavior and has been transformed by requirements of love and marriage. Leaving man free in the sexual arena does not solve the problem. It makes the concept of chastity/morality even more complicated.

Let us give another example. Let's apply scientific methodology in the process of solving social relationships. Let us organize these relationships with prior planning such that everything will be placed exactly where it is supposed to be as per the overall design, and, thus, everyone and everything will move and work exactly as per the scientific plan. In this way, if all the pieces perform as they are supposed to, no problems should arise. Order will rule; no one will be permitted to trespass the pre-determined limits of his activities; each piece will work in complete harmony with the rest. In this way, human society will become a machine-like organization. But, man is not a machine; man is not a honey bee, is not an ant or a termite. He cannot constantly perform a specific task within inviolable limits. Sooner or later his taste and talent will emerge and necessitate expression. In order to keep man within his limits he must be forced to conform. The political orders, which aim to transform human society into beehives or ant nests, hope to make animals out of human beings; such systems must impose the most tyrannical political autocracies upon their people to ensure conformity. Such a system would remove the possibility of deviation

138

from the norm and would keep everyone within the circle of his designed roles; in so doing, nothing that is human will survive.

To establish such systems much blood has been shed, and yet the process continues. All of this regimentation is the result of attempting to organize human life on the basis of reason and science. Proponents of the scientific process forget that human problems cannot be solved in this way. If the element of religious Faith is unheeded by reason and science, that work within their own limits, humanness will lose it meaning altogether.

Therefore, the compatibility of science and religion does not mean that whatever religion ordains is followed by science or, conversely, what science decrees is what religion has to abide by. In other words, neither can take the place of the other. Each has a distinct arena of activity and should not trespass into the other's sphere. Science and the intellect are free to perform their work. Scientific pronouncements are recognized as reliable and trustworthy. In fact, adoption of ones religious belief nowadays is dependent upon reason; this is different from the former practices which acknowledged the use of the mind only as long as the mind believed what it was told to believe under penalty of death.

In the Bahá'í Faith each person is encouraged to find the religious belief he wishes to adopt based on the dictates of his own reason and heart. One may wish to become a Bahá'í or not; none has the right to question or object to that decision. What is also significant is that religious rules of worship, rituals and customs have been reduced. Religious requirements of belief and acts of worship have decreased. Details of personal religious duties and obligations have not been prescribed and have been left to the individual so that he may make such decision in accordance with his own common sense. All Local Spiritual Assemblies have been given instructions by the Guardian that their pronouncements to the community should be general in nature and, to the extent possible, should not interfere in the personal lives of the friends.

Even regarding the most important pillar of the Faith namely the authority and rank of Bahá'u'lláh, He, in one of His tablets, openly declares that:

"Each person is free to make such recognition according to his own conscience as long as he would not try to impose his understanding upon others. And if two people argue over such a point neither viewpoint would be acceptable since they wish to impose their view as an excuse to teach the Faith and this is the very essence of error."[5]

In this way religion accepts the rule of reason and science, and reason and science, too, accept the rule of religion. The two not only become compatible but collaborative; in this way both can endure and guarantee the survival of the human race. That is what the human race desires.

---

[5] For the original text of the verse see the Tablet to Jamál (untranslated); also see the book *Iqtidárát* (untranslated).

13. The Essentiality of Religion

It is generally believed that in animals instinct is the governing and controlling factor behind all actions, conditions and movements. The concept of the "animal instinct" has been the cause of much discussion and controversy; however our purpose here is not to take up any such investigation or study but only briefly treat the subject as an opening statement to the discussion of the essentiality of religion.

Instinct, in animals, is the director of all their movements and actions. Similar to the parts of any machine, every part in animals performs in accordance with a pre-determined set of rules and achieves its designed purpose without any controlling intention on the part of the animal; such a controlling intention could lead to results different from the one the part is destined to achieve. Even if, at times, a small deviation from this pre-determined process is noted, the deviation is within certain limits which the animal can never hope to breach. Because of this lack of total control, the concept of good and evil plays no part in animal life. Moral training has no meaning here unless man enters the picture and wishes to train the animal to satisfy his own pleasure. Even such training is not considered natural since the rule of nature is that the animal should be guided in a prescribed direction, on a predetermined course, towards a predestined end. Therefore, we are unable to determine the difference of "means" and "goals" in animals. In point of fact, all acts and movements of the animal are both "means" and "goals";

in the animal kingdom means and goals are common; thus, every action can be seen as means to a goal or the goal itself.

In man, it is a different story. Man's goals are not predetermined. He is not obligated to actually set any goals and realize such goals in a prescribed manner and on a predetermined course. In man, priorities emerge, and preference for one choice over the others dictates the course of action he follows. Things, as man considers them, are transformed into values. In its relation to man every "thing" will assume a "value" or "worth". and Since there is a relationship between the realities of things, the values that are so defined also become related; a cluster or clusters of values come into existence, and man is presented with a choice to accept the value cluster that he finds most suitable and befitting. Having made such a selection, he then determines the means for achieving the goal which his choice of a value cluster has set before him. The will power that uniquely exists in him and which he exercises to choose his goals and the intellect that determines the means to attain them differentiates his condition from the unalterable, inviolable and inevitable conditions that govern the animal. This major transformation between animal and man is generally regarded as the replacement of instinct by intellect or the extension of instinctive perception into intellectual determination in a human being.

So what is the role of the mind or the intellect? The mind discovers an unknown based on premises that are known. Intellect is simply a means or a tool that maps out the route from the known to the unknown. The mind does not set goals; it devises the way to achieve goals. The identity of the goal is of little consequence to the mind; it simply finds a way to realize the goal. Suppose one wants to commit burglary. His goal is to steal someone else's property. The mind readily places itself at his disposal in order to discover the best way to achieve the goal. The greatest crimes in the world community are carried out through the complete participation of the intellectual power. A physician uses the same intellectual capacity to heal the sick. The politician, the merchant and the housewife also use the same intellect to reach their aims. The point is that the mind remains completely indifferent to the task it is being called to perform. Its job is to bring a person step by step closer to the goal he has set until the goal is realized.

If intellect is the process by which goals are achieved, let us find out what power determines or sets the goals. The goals are not determined by the mind since the goals are not fixed or clearly defined; they are dependent on the value or the worth that the individual attaches to things. In other words, things must be given values, upon which the goals and the priority of their achievements are determined. These values are those that man adopts or attaches to things that he feels are "good" and of benefit to him. The nature of goals to be achieved cannot be dictated by an innate concept of goodness or evil. if this were the case man, would have emerged as a higher order of the animal whose goals had been pre-determined and personal selection and choice would have no meaning. However, we can readily see that two individuals can have opposing views regarding the "goodness" of the same goal: a goal that may seem "good "to one could be seen as "evil" to another.

Thus, we arrive at the conclusion that man can choose the goals of his life as he wishes and may claim that such freedom to choose is purely dictated by the power of his intellect. One could pose the question whether or not the intellect is also capable of selecting the right path for achieving the goal. If it is so, then there should be no conflict between individuals about the goals that are set or the paths that are chosen to achieve them. However, that is not the case: the goals are different, and people do not adopt the same approaches for the realization of these goals. The concepts of good and evil are considered differently by different people. While a goal and the path to its realization may seem right to me, you may consider both to be wrong and would propose a totally different solution. In such a case how can we determine who is right and who is not? We both have sound intellects, sound knowledge and good intentions. So who is right? I claim that I recognize the "good" and the "bad" when I choose to be good and am capable of setting the right goals and selecting the right approach, why should I have a need for any other guidance? If I consider your goal and approach as wrong, then whose diagnosis should determine the way forward? Such disagreements can, over time, reach the stage of hostility and coercion of one view over the other which reduces us to the level of the animal. Thus, it becomes necessary that another factor or determinant dictates the nature of the goals being set so that the mind can step in and devise the path to its attainment. Some believe that such a determinant is the judgment of the scholars, the philosophers, or the savants. However, we see that the scholars are also of different and, at times, conflicting views regarding any one given issue. What is to be done, then? It seems that the true recognition of the concepts of good and evil must originate from a different source. The adoption of appropriate goals, dreams and aspirations based on this difference source would lead to the proper guidance of the intellect to determine the way forward.

Every intellect follows a certain pattern, is more efficient in a certain environment, can work within certain limits of time and space, and under specified conditions and requirements. Because of this the intellect of man is called the minor intellect. A dominant, universal and overpowering Intellect is required to determine the ultimate goals, and then, within such an overall goal, the minor intellects can pave the way for the realization of the smaller aims and targets that together will move humanity towards that ultimate goal.

We need to accept the pronouncements of this universal Intellect; if we reject these pronouncements we will be confronted with the same confusion and chaos that opposing views of small intellects generate which will eventually lead to divisions of thought, differences of beliefs, hostility and ultimately war. We have to admit to the imperfection of our own intellects and establish a connection

144

between our minor intellects and that perfect and Universal one. With such a connection we consider ourselves to be religious. In other words, religious belief is nothing more than accepting the connection between our intellect and the Universal Intellect so that we are enabled to choose the right "value clusters", select the right goals, and follow the right approach to their realization.

Acceptance of religious belief emerges as an essential requirement of life; however, there is an additional argument. While man's intellect can guide him in the right direction, he still may decide not to walk that path and instead may choose to follow his own whim and desire even if it is clearly against his own common sense and understanding of what he knows to be right.

Socrates taught that righteousness comes from knowledge. In other words, if one knows the difference between good and bad, he will choose the good and eschew the bad: thus, righteousness is nothing but the awareness of the limits of good and evil. We, therefore, conclude that those who do evil are those who know not what they do. This leads to the conclusion that knowledge is righteousness. Knowledge is the dictate of the intellect; it can be said that the designations of intellect and righteousness essentially imply the same thing. Of course, this argument is only true if by intellect we mean the Universal Intellect. It is clear that if the concept of the mutual identity of righteousness and intellect is applied to man's intellect, the same conclusion cannot be reached. A good example of the dichotomy between the two forces is a physician who while better informed than others of the evils of smoking and drinking yet himself smokes and drinks.

If knowledge were, in fact, righteousness, then no physician would be expected to smoke, drink and consume greasy foods. Yet, that is not the case; we can clearly see that the judgment of the personal intellect is incapable of helping man to reach his goals even if the intellect could achieve the highest knowledge. The only contribution of the personal intellect is to organize the means to realize the goal that has already been fixed. In other words, even if the intellect had the power to set goals, it does not necessarily follow that a man would choose to tread a specific path to reach the goal. Aside from the intellect's role in goal setting, it becomes essential to pursue a goal for man with which he himself is in agreement. That gap between the goal set by the intellect and the path man chooses to follow is controlled by Faith. Faith operates in the same arena as personal intellect and is not in conflict with the Universal Intellect. In fact, Faith is of the same essence and forms a connection between man and the Universal Intellect.

However, if we look at the personal intellect, we will note that, at times, it may appear to be in conflict with Faith. In such a case reliance on the power of Faith, which reflects the power of love or the power of emotion, becomes essential; the intellect may be placed at the service of Faith and produce the means of attaining a given goal. Faith, then, is a force that like a rope pulls the individual in the right direction although his desire may drive him in the wrong direction. Thus, once the determination of good and evil is made dependent upon the connection of man to the Universal Intellect (which can be referred to as Faith and is an element of religion), then there is no question of compliance or non-compliance, no further concern of advantage or disadvantage, of benefit or loss.

Why is this so? Because the selection of "goodness" has been established through connection with the Universal Intellect or the Universal Mind, or in simpler terms, it is because God has established the goal, and as a true believer we follow the path for its realization. If such a connection becomes universal it obviates the need for the existence of police, supervisors or controllers.

Of course, it cannot be denied that man possesses a moral conscience which can naturally or instinctively provide him with the distinction between good and evil. We must, however, admit that such a power exists in people at different levels of intensity; even so, man is capable of interpreting the decree of his conscience and coming up with justifications, rational or otherwise, to do what he pleases. Suppose one wishes to accept a bribe for performing a service. His conscience tells him it is a wrong thing to do. Yet he is able to justify the act by assuring himself that although such an act is not right, yet not only will the briber achieves his purpose but he, too, will receive the funds necessary to pay for the education of his child, and once the child is educated he may be able to help many people. In other words, he finds so many advantages for committing a single wrongdoing that he is ultimately able to change the nature of the "wrong doing" into a "right doing" in his conscience; nay, rather the former 'wrong-doing' becomes a duty and a responsibility. Thus, we see that the decree of the conscience can lend itself to misinterpretation and misdirection. What is certain is that once man's conscience is reinforced by the power of Faith, it will flourish and becomes more pronounced and manifest. He whose conscience is feeble and sluggish derives from Faith strength, courage, energy and firmness, and he whose conscience is already strong becomes even more substantial and forceful. What is clear is that Faith in the Universal Intellect makes man a more powerful being. This positive effect of Faith is true if we consider the existence of conscience in man as an instinctive phenomenon. However, even if we admit to the lack of such a power in some people, Bahá'u'lláh has told us that, in man there exists a mental tendency called "shame" that exhorts him towards "good" and warns him against "evil".[1] Obviously such a tendency is not shared by all in the same measure. However, for

---

[1] The exact text of Bahá'u'lláh in Ishráqát (Splendors) is as follows: *first leaf* of the Most Exalted Paradise is this: Verily I say: The fear of God hath ever been a sure defense and a safe stronghold for all the peoples of the world. It is the chief cause of the protection of mankind, and the supreme instrument for its preservation. Indeed, there existeth in man a faculty which deterreth him from, and guardeth him against, whatever is unworthy and unseemly, and which is known as his sense of shame. This, however, is confined to but a few; all have not possessed and do not possess it.

those who do possess shame, such an instinct is strengthened and reinforced in those who are endowed with the gift of Faith.

From a different viewpoint, Faith in a Universal Mind and man's connection with such a source bestows upon him the belief in life eternal or conversely removes from him the fear that life is limited to what is within the bounds of time and space. There is a difference between an individual who considers his life to have started at birth and to end at death and the individual who considers his life to be eternal. The person who believes is constantly moving towards his annihilation with death becomes more and more depressed, gloomy and remorseful for not having achieved in life what he had planned or having failed to experience the joys and pleasures of life as others might have done. Despair and hopelessness gradually take from him the ability to enjoy what life has to offer. Whereas to the person who believes in eternal life, death is simply a turn in the road of life, an end to a particular period and a beginning of a new experience. And as he is aware of the nature of life's extension after the death of the body, he passes his life with joy and contentment. This state of happiness which is the result of his reliance on the power of his Faith remains with him until the end of his physical existence.

When man arrives at such a conviction and his reliance on the power of Faith becomes strong, the world will become another world. It would be pure joy to live in such a world. We are constantly moving towards such a world and are getting closer and closer all the time, and if we, in our lifetime, do not reach the goal, as our lives are eternal, surely we will witness the arrival of that day and will experience the joy of seeing our loved ones embracing such a delight in the days to come.

14. Philosophy and Religion

When we speak of the philosophy of religion, understanding of two concepts becomes essential. One concept to understand is the circumstances attending the appearance of religion, to understand the world conditions which may have given rise to its emergence. The second necessary concept is to appreciate the universality of religion's spiritual principles and intellectual concepts which appeal to the seeker, captivate his mind and soul and transform him to such a state that he can embrace these aspects of religion and become a believer. In the ideal transformation the seeker would willingly acknowledge such concepts as God, soul, matter and the eternal world in accordance with the revealed precepts of the religion and accept to conform to the moral, ethical and social principles these concepts inculcate.

Philosophy is not only basic to the fundamentals of religion. It is also the defining basis of all areas and conditions of human life in the world of existence. The subject of this talk is religious philosophy which is the collection of the basic principles of religion defining such concepts as God, soul, the origin of the world of creation, the destiny of man, and the meaning of this contingent world.

Religious philosophy that attracts its adherents and commits them to upholding its tenets while renouncing all similar and competing interpretations or alternatives is the subject of a long story, and each religion has its own chronicles and adventures. In the East it can readily be seen that philosophy has always emerged out of religious concepts, and, indeed, philosophy independent of revealed religion has not existed. For example, in China philosophy and religion are inseparable, and the same is true in India. In ancient Persia, too, every philosophical movement had its religious dimension.

The country in which philosophy flourished independently and was not only separate from religion but at times in conflict with it is Greece, the birthplace of Western Civilization. The philosophers of this country pursued a thought process that fell outside of the conventional flow of religious orthodoxy. Socrates and his followers discussed philosophical themes that carried within them seeds of science in the form of scientific theories separate from religious concepts.

It should be noted that at first these two approaches of religion and philosophy were inseparable, however gradually each went its own way and they became independent concepts. For example, in the works of Plato one can see ideas regarding life, soul, origin of creation and resurrection without the adoption of any ideas from the teachings of religion. In other words the ideas of the Greek philosophers regarding these concepts and even their ideas about God, religion and the eternal world were predicated on intellectual examination and logical evaluation, independent of belief in any religious revelation or divine Faith.

Although the influence of religious concepts on philosophical teachings of Plato and his contemporaries is undeniable, this should not imply that there was any attempt on their part to express views that were consistent with the principles of religion or any intention of molding philosophy after religion. Admittedly, Greek philosophers were inspired by religious teachings, but they proposed these ideas, that persisted until the appearance of

Christianity, solely on the basis of the dialectical and rational merits of the ideas.

Christianity, after centuries of obscurity, achieved recognition and began expanding westward until it came face to face with this rival intellectual environment. The rivalry originated in the attempt by the philosophers of the day to shed light on many cryptic religious concepts through the application of logic. The Old and New Testaments contain chronicles on the creation of the world, the creation of Adam, the appearance of Jesus, His martyrdom for the salvation of mankind and the concept of the second coming. Christians believed that understanding of such events could only emanate from divine revelation. However, the philosophers examined these issues through the application of reason and arrived at conclusions that were inconsistent with those adhered to by the religionists. This difference of viewpoint led to dispute, conflict and, ultimately, to hostility between the two groups. Eventually, on the instruction of Justinian, the Christian Emperor of the Eastern Roman Empire, all of Greece's centers of philosophical learning were closed. As a result, a number of Greek philosophers sought refuge at the court of the Persian Emperor Khosrau II.

With Justinian's action, religion made its very first assault upon philosophy. Although prior conflicts had existed between the two groups, yet it had always been of a minor nature. However this time, the hostilities expanded to such dimensions that no century of the Middle Ages was free from Christianity's denunciation and reprobation of philosophy.

The basic cause behind the conflict was the Christian's view that man was incapable of unraveling spiritual mysteries through the use of intellect alone; the philosophers pronounced that the human mind was the only portal through which man could arrive at the resolution of such mysteries. Some individuals succeeded in reconciling the two sides and delineating Christian beliefs on the basis of Greek philosophical thought; in this way the Bible could find acceptability through both reason and Faith. The first steps towards Christian philosophy were being taken.

The early attempts at reconciliation were greeted with utter disdain by the church, and those who were involved in such rapprochement received harsh punishments. However, the process continued to grow, and a few centuries after the ascendency of Christianity across the European continent, philosophy finally found a place within the Christian belief system; the church finally came to credit Greek thought, and the foundation of Christian philosophy was laid.

Following this, suddenly there was a major about face in church practices. The ideas which had been previously abhorred and rejected by the church gained acceptance and ultimately became the official doctrine of Christian teachings. This transformation was due to the acknowledgement, by the church fathers, of Aristotelian philosophy as interpreted by an Italian Christian scholar, Thomas Aquinas.

The Jews had made a similar effort at reconciling Jewish teachings with Greek rational thought. A Jewish scholar, Philon, took on the challenge of harmonizing the principles of the Torah with Greek philosophy. He strived to explain and interpret the stories and tales of the Holy Book, especially the topics of creationism, the fall of man from grace and other cryptic concepts which he had considered figurative or allegorical. The views of Philon did not find acceptance within the Jewish ecclesiastical hierarchy; nevertheless, religious scholars did not give up this challenge and continued to explore interpretive approaches looking for areas of agreement between their views. Among these scholars, Avicebron was the most prominent.

Greek philosophy found its way into the Islamic world through Arabic translations by Muslim linguists. The collision and conflict of intellect and religion emerged in Islam as it had in Christianity and Judaism. At first, the followers of the philosophical approach were rejected and excommunicated. Later, over time, some of them found acceptance. Each Islamic sect derived a different benefit from the teachings of the Greek scholars, and gradually Greek philosophy developed in two distinct areas. One led to the emergence of such great thinkers as Farabi and Avicenna who arranged and presented philosophical views free from religious doctrines, although they were careful not to express thoughts contrary to Islamic laws and tenets. If these scholars detected any conflicts between the their views and Islamic laws, they either acquiesced or offered some sort of justification.

The development of Greek philosophy also led to the appearance of scholars who wished to express philosophy on the basis of religious belief. These scholars adopted Islam as the fundamental truth and built upon it what came to be known as Islamic philosophy. These thinkers were referred to as the "people of the Word" or the "Speakers". They strived to provide logical explanations for religious teachings such as "the return", "reality and qualities of God" and other such abstruse concepts.

The greatest of these, whose rank among the Islamic Sunnis may be comparable to that of Thomas Aquinas among the Catholics, is Abul-Hassan 'Ash'ari. This sage, as well as others who followed his philosophy (such as Muhammad Ghazáli), felt that certain principles must be devised to ascertain God's role as the absolute Creator and his omnipotent Will as the source of all created things, including man's destiny. Furthermore, God's absolute knowledge of the minutest details or events of this contingent world should be openly acknowledged; God's will should be recognized as the only effective and motivating factor in the world of creation, without the requirement of any intellectual clarification or mediation from any scholar or arbiter. In this way, certain definitive and authoritative principles emerged in Islamic philosophy which found acceptance in the community.

In the Islamic world, philosophical views were greeted with disdain by the clergy and the ruling class; in some cases, the falsity of these views was openly and fiercely declared, raising a storm of condemnation and denunciation which lead to arrests and excommunications. One such case was the controversy surrounding the nature of the Qur'an. Was the Qur'an revealed in time or was it pre-existent? This argument created a horrific uproar of dissention and clash of doctrines. Once 'Ash'ari's philosophy, which lies at the basis of Sunni belief, was acknowledged, things calmed down and agreement was established. (He proposed that the words were contingent and the meanings eternal-Translator)

The Shi'ite sect of Islam entered this arena rather late. As a minor branch of Islam it remained incoherent and disorganized even after some nine hundred years following the appearance of Islam. However, once the Shi'ite sect became the national religion of Persia, the dispute between religion and philosophy grew into a major controversy which led to many condemnations and excommunications. Strange to say, today, Ash'ari's philosophy is also considered by the literate among the population as the "philosophy of Shi'ite Islam".

Such philosophical controversies which have been at the root of so much conflict and dispute in previous religions have no place in the Bahá'í Faith. This era in the Bahá'í Faith is the period of learning, deepening, teaching, proclamation, propagation and pioneering. It is the period of action, prosecution and creation. It is the time of spiritual campaign and expansion of Bahá'í principles in the four corners of the world.

However, for the generation of Bahá'í philosophical literature that will clearly set forth the teachings of the Faith and which will express the collective understanding of the people of Bahá of the Writings of the Exalted Pen, Bahá'u'lláh, one must look to future centuries; at such a time engaging in scholarly studies will not interfere with teaching efforts and pioneering activities. Furthermore, such scholarly works will be most effective when the entirety of the Writings of the Herald, the Author and the interpreters of the Faith, the volume of which in terms of its diversity, expanse, majesty and sublimity is immense, have been studied, analyzed and published and the realization of its prophecies have, in the course of time, been demonstrated. At such a time, the study and instruction of such sacred Writings in a proper manner and in formal centers of research under the guidance of the Universal House of Justice will take place and the scholars of the Faith, free from public hindrances, will present the results of their investigations in scientific and literary assemblies and seminars. These activities will serve as the preamble for the emergence of scholars and philosophers in whose honor Bahá'u'lláh has revealed the following in the Tablet of Wisdom:

"Verily We love those men of knowledge who have brought to light such things as promote the best interests of humanity, and We aided them through the potency of Our behest, for well are We able to achieve Our purpose."

CPSIA information can be obtained
at www.ICGtesting.com
Printed in the USA
LVOW03s0205190717
541845LV00001B/148/P